New Ways in Teaching Grammar

Edited by Martha C. Pennington

New Ways in TESOL Series
Innovative Classroom Techniques
Jack C. Richards, Series Editor
Teachers of English to Speakers of Other Languages, Inc.

Typeset in Garamond Book and Tiffany Demi
by Automated Graphic Systems, White Plains, Maryland
and printed by
Pantagraph Printing, Bloomington, Illinois USA

Teachers of English to Speakers of Other Languages, Inc.
1600 Cameron Street, Suite 300
Alexandria, Virginia 22314 USA
Tel 703-836-0774 • Fax 703-836-7864

Director of Communications and Marketing: Helen Kornblum
Senior Editor: Marilyn Kupetz
Editorial Assistant: Cheryl Donnelly
Cover Design and Spot Art: Ann Kammerer
Part Title Illustrations: David Connell

ISBN 0-939791-56-0
Library of Congress Catalogue No. 94-061424

065099

Contents

Acknowledgments

This edited collection has been, in many senses, a collective effort involving the ideas, skills, work, and cooperation of many individuals. As editor and on behalf of all of the contributors, I want to express our appreciation, first of all, to Marilyn Kupetz and the TESOL Central Office staff for their editorial guidance and for their creative and technical assistance in the editing and production of the book. The overall format, the graphics, and the detailed production of the whole New Ways in Teaching series are the result of their creative and professional efforts. I would also like to thank Jack Richards for his inspiration and ideas for the volume.

The book also owes a great debt to several people in the English Department office at City Polytechnic of Hong Kong. Thanks are due in particular to Carmen Cheng Yin Ling, who served as my editorial assistant on the project. Carmen was in charge of managing and filing all incoming contributions, updating the contributor list and table of contents, converting files, making copies, typing submissions of contributors who did not have access to a word processor, and incorporating editorial changes submitted by me or by the authors. Thanks are due as well to other members of the English Department office staff who assisted Carmen in carrying out her responsibilities on the project. They are: Eva Cheung Lai Fong, Heidi Lam Kwai Chun, Kitty Leung Yin Fan, Jackie Tang Chiu Fung, and Miranda Yung Yee Wa. The energetic and efficient assistance of these individuals has been essential to the ongoing management and completion of this project.

This book could also not have been completed without the patience and assistance of the 56 people who submitted activities and who cooperated with me in revising their contributions over a 2-year period. I thank all of these colleagues and friends for their creativity, their energy, and their support in bringing this project to a successful conclusion and bringing together what I believe is an interesting and useful reference for teachers of English to speakers of other languages around the globe.

Introduction: Toward an Enriched View of the Teaching of Grammar

This book includes 85 ideas for the teaching of grammar submitted by English teachers from 10 countries in Asia, Europe, North America, and South America. The contributions have been divided into 10 major sections that include specific aspects of grammar such as noun phrases and modal verbs, as well as grammar topics at the discourse level, such as question-and-answer patterns and activities for editing and revising written texts. One of the major sections contains general purpose activities that can be applied broadly in different areas of grammar. Cross reference is also made in the Users' Guide to Activities to activities in other sections that are relevant to the topic of a particular section. In addition, with a little imagination, many of the activities of this book can be adapted for areas of grammar other than those they were intended to practice.

Most of the contributions are short—only a few pages each—and by design include little if any discussion of grammatical theory or educational philosophy. Yet a clear philosophy emerges from the collection. Though the contributions are extremely diverse in the areas of grammar addressed and the specific teaching techniques advocated, they are nevertheless all based on a similar contemporary amalgam of ideas, or theme, about grammar teaching and learning. The theme that ties together this collection can be labeled a *situated process* perspective on language education. In what follows, I will attempt to describe how this theme plays itself out in the views of grammar learning and grammar teaching represented in this volume and in the field of teaching English to speakers of other languages more generally.

A Situated Process View of Grammar Learning

For a long time, many students and teachers of English language have operated under a static conception of language centered on a limited view of grammar. In this limited view, grammar is seen, paradoxically, as the heart of language and at the same time as manifested in restricted and controlled production of correct sentences, based on a relatively formal and academic norm for written language. In spite of Chomsky's (1957) introduction of the concept of two levels of grammar, deep structure and surface structure, and of later developments in discourse grammar (deBeaugrande, 1980; Brown & Yule, 1983), the notion of learning grammar as learning to produce accurate surface forms in the minimal context of a sentence or single utterance already planned somehow outside the domain of grammar has persisted. (For additional discussion of this point, see Lock, forthcoming.)

This collection of grammar teaching ideas is based on a richer and more substantial conception of grammar: one that realizes the meaning potential of language through multiple interlocking or interdependent grammatical systems (Halliday, 1985; Rutherford, 1987). This polysystemic orientation implies that there is not in fact only one correct form of the grammar of a language but rather a range of options useful for different purposes and appropriate in different situations. From this point of view, grammar is not a set structure but a flexible frame with interchangeable components that can be organized and manipulated in different ways. By manipulating linguistic components within a grammatical frame, speakers are able to produce a wide variety of constructions to meet their own communicative needs and the requirements of different audiences and genres.

In this view, grammar is more a matter of selection than correction. Grammar is, in other words, about selecting the appropriate option(s) from a range of possibilities, rather than simply recalling and producing—or reproducing—language in one particular form, that is, the one prescribed by the grammar teacher or another authoritative source. Because from this perspective grammar is a process of choosing forms and constructing language in response to communicative demands, it essentially involves the learner's creative response to context and circumstance. The philosophy of this book is therefore one that moves away from the traditional prescriptive grammar of written sentences and towards a situated grammar of spoken and written discourse.

The orientation of the present volume is thus quite different from the traditional product-based conception of grammar as a human artifact—something that can be set down between the covers of a book and learned alone through diligent effort—that is, the rules and prescriptions of a grammar text. The view of grammar as a product of human experience and tradition is here superseded by a process-based conception in which grammar is seen as a dynamic shaping force in the ever-changing context and process of communication. Through the communicative process in which meaning is negotiated and expressed, grammar evolves and shapes a situated discourse or text.

Not only the use of grammar, but also the learning of grammar is properly viewed as a process. Rather than focusing on the acquisition of grammar as an event, the process perspective on grammatical acquisition is a long-term focus in which the learner's interim achievements, temporary behaviors, and progress over time are central concerns. A major difference between a product and a process view of grammar learning is the emphasis in the latter on the gradual and progressive nature of learning (Rutherford, 1987).

In the process conception, acquiring grammatical knowledge involves actively and creatively constructing the grammar from the information that is known to and available to the learner (Dulay & Burt, 1976, 1977). As part of this creative process, in which the learner actively attempts to extract regularities from what she or he hears or reads in the L2 and to produce a grammar with limited information, errors will occur. Given enough time and enough opportunities to communicate and to receive feedback on attempts at producing meaningful language, these errors will gradually diminish, as the learner continually reanalyzes, adjusts, and elaborates the mental grammar to bring it more into line with the grammatical system of the L2 (Corder, 1981; Selinker, 1972, 1992).

In addition, what is unconsciously absorbed by natural acquisition processes is refined by knowledge learned consciously (Krashen, 1981, 1982). It may also be possible for what is learned consciously to gradually become unconscious and automatic, that is, fluent performance. To become skilled language users for whom performance is fluent and automatic (McLaughlin, 1987), learners need considerable practice over a considerable period of time.

As a human process, grammatical acquisition is both intellectual and affective in nature. In order for the unconscious processes of acquisition to operate, learners must not only be exposed to a rich learning environment but must also be in a favorable psychological state (Dulay & Burt, 1977; Krashen, 1981, 1982). They must also be motivated—whether instrumentally or integratively (Gardner, 1985; Gardner & Lambert, 1972)—and invested in learning.

In addition to its psychological aspect, grammar learning viewed as a process has a social aspect in that learning to use a language means learning to interact with other communicators. As learners increase their interest in and their need to communicate with different individuals for different purposes, they require additional communicative resources. Language learners elaborate their linguistic system in response to communicative need and the requirements of different audiences and purposes of communication, as these are revealed to them through feedback on performance. Where needs are minimal or artificial, so is the learner's grammatical system, producing simplifications and fossilized error types (Corder, 1981).

The grammar learning process is situated in the contexts of human meaning and human society. Thus, learners acquire additional grammatical resources and a more elaborated knowledge of grammar as a way to express themselves more precisely as they intend, more deeply and creatively, and in more diverse types of discourse. By continually developing their grammatical system, learners may achieve the point at which they can employ the L2 for the full range of functions and intricate meaning differences which they are capable of imagining—perhaps even beyond those which they are able to express in their L1.

A Situated Process View of Grammar Teaching

Based on the foregoing discussion, a central goal for grammar pedagogy will be for the learner to build up, over time, a grammatical repertoire and an understanding of the functions of that grammatical repertoire in various contexts of communication. For successful language use, the learner will also need to acquire the ability to apply various grammatical structures in responding to the demands of audience and communicational context. Language learners therefore need not only to be exposed to the structures and functions of communication but also to practice applying grammatical knowledge in real-time contexts and to receive feedback on the effectiveness of their attempts to construct discourse that communicates their intentions.

When grammar is taught and practiced as a means of communication, rather than as a means for correcting the mechanics and surface accuracy of sentences, it becomes a more purposeful and therefore a more motivating focus for classroom learning. As the purpose and realization of grammar become less artificial, the application of grammar in the classroom becomes more open-ended and creative. In this way, the practice of grammar comes to represent a more essential kind of language activity, involving the creative construction of meaningful discourse in response to the exigencies of face-to-face interaction and communication within various discourse communities.

The activities of this book recognize the importance of motivation in grammar pedagogy, as in all learning and teaching. Indeed, it is motivation, through "choice, engagement, and persistence, as determined by interest, relevance, expectancy, and outcomes" (Crookes & Schmidt, 1991, p. 502), that drives the whole learning process. Accordingly, instructional approaches for teaching ESOL grammar ought to be based on general principles of effective instruction that consider the features of learners' interests and goals, interactional dynamics and classroom climate, and appropriate feedback and reward systems. By considering motivational characteristics such as these, instructional approaches for grammar make classroom input as *accessible* as possible—that is, understandable, relevant, and salient—thereby ensuring that the input is as interpretable, memorable, and useful as possible.

Motivation and accessibility of input are provided in the present volume by activities that:

- attend to communicative need and purpose
- place grammatical structures in real or realistic contexts
- make creative use of various sorts of everyday objects, visual aids, and special-purpose graphics
- incorporate humor or other highly motivating content
- provide challenge and interest through gamelike features
- promote choice, independence, creativity, realism, and feedback through pair and small-group work.

The ability to choose and apply grammatical concepts appropriately are also encouraged by activities to raise grammatical consciousness and develop skills for reflection and self-assessment.

The activities of this book offer language teachers a wealth of ideas to motivate learners' interest and sustain their attention in the long-term process of acquiring grammatical knowledge and skills in English. They also offer ample opportunities to practice and use grammar realistically and meaningfully so as to activate learners' knowledge and increase the fluency and automaticity of their performance. In adding to the opportunities for meaningful practice and interaction, they enhance the social aspect of classroom language learning, thereby further increasing the realism and usefulness of grammar lessons.

The activities of this book offer teachers increased resources for incorporating a grammatical focus in the language classroom in ways that will give learners increased opportunities and motivation to interact with other communicators, to raise their awareness of the forms and functions of English grammar, to incorporate various grammatical structures in their performance, and to elaborate and refine these in relation to communicative demands. These activities thus have the potential for changing the grammar classroom from a place where the teacher corrects the learner's performance into an environment in which the learner's grammatical system is elaborated by the dynamics of the communicative process, and performance is enhanced by raising the level of grammatical awareness. In this way, use of the activities in this volume might increase the creativity and variety of the repertoires and skills of language learners and language teachers, helping to make grammar instruction a valuable and enjoyable enterprise for all concerned.

In developing this book, every effort has been made to solicit the best possible ideas from the widest possible group of educators in the teaching of English to speakers of other languages. As a result, the material spans a great range of types of activities designed to motivate and provide practice opportunities for language learners from beginning to advanced levels of proficiency. Consistent with the prevailing principles and practices of our field, these activities incorporate learner-centered, cooperative, reflective, and communicative orientations to language teaching. If there are still gaps in the book, either in subject matter or types of activities, this presumably represents gaps in our collective consciousness of grammar—gaps that will presumably be filled as our field continues to broaden and deepen its perspectives on language teaching.

References

deBeauregrande, R. (1980). *Text, discourse and process.* London: Longman.

Brown, G., & Yule, G. (1983). *Discourse analysis.* Cambridge: Cambridge University Press.

Chomsky, N. (1957). *Syntactic structures.* The Hague: Mouton.

Corder, S. P. (1981). *Error analysis and interlanguage.* Oxford: Oxford University Press.

Crookes, G., & Schmidt, R. W. (1991). Motivation: Reopening the research agenda. *Language Learning, 41,* 469-512.

Dulay, H., & Burt, M. K. (1976). Creative construction in second language learning and teaching. *Language Learning, 4,* 65-79.

Dulay, H., & Burt, M. K. (1977). Remarks on creativity in language acquisition. In M. Burt, H. Dulay, & M. Finochiaro (Eds.), *Viewpoints on English as a second language* (pp. 95-96). New York: Regents.

Gardner, R. C. (1985). *Social psychology and second language learning: The role of attitudes and motivation.* London: Edward Arnold.

Gardner, R. C., & Lambert, W. (1972). *Attitudes and motivation in second language learning.* Rowley, MA: Newbury House.

Halliday, M. A. K. (1985). *An introduction to functional grammar.* London: Edward Arnold.

Krashen, S. D. (1981). *Second language acquisition and second language learning.* Oxford: Pergamon.

Krashen, S. D. (1982). *Principles and practice in second language acquisition.* Oxford: Pergamon.

Lock, G. (forthcoming). Some issues in the learning and teaching of a grammar. In *Functional English grammar for language teachers.* New York: Cambridge University Press.

McLaughlin, B. (1987). *Theories of second language learning.* London: Edward Arnold.

Rutherford, W. (1987). *Second language grammar: Learning and teaching.* London: Longman.

Selinker, L. (1972). Interlanguage. *International Review of Applied Linguistics, 10,* 209-231.

Selinker, L. (1992). *Rediscovering interlanguage.* London: Longman.

Users' Guide to Activities

Part III: Tenses

Present Tense

Past Tense

Present Perfect

Past Perfect

Conditionals

Sequence of Tenses

General Tenses

Part IV: Modal Verbs

Part V: Verb Complements

Part VI: Passive Voice and Ergative Verbs

Part VII: Adverbs and Adverbial Clauses

Part VIII: Questions and Answers

Part I: Noun Phrases and Clauses

◆ Adjectives and Nouns
Noun Phrase Mix Up

Levels
Beginning

Aims
Recognize the syntactic
structure of a noun
phrase (article +
adjective + noun) by
associating physical
order with syntactic
structure

Class Time
10–15 minutes

Preparation Time
10 minutes

Resources
Index cards

Students physically create noun phrases by matching appropriate elements in several ways.

Procedure

1. Think of noun phrases within the students' vocabulary and write each article, adjective, and noun on a separate card. If the class cannot easily be divided by three, include extra adjectives.
2. Give each student one card that they may not show the others.
3. Students circulate around the room asking others the content of their card until they find two other students who have a part of a noun phrase they lack. (e.g., A student with a noun would be looking for students with an article and an adjective.)
4. When three students have the components to create a noun phrase, they form a group, standing in correct noun phrase order.
5. Have each group tell their noun phrase to the class. The phrases may be written on the board.
6. The groups disburse and circulate again, forming new noun phrases.
7. Repeat Step 5.

Caveats and Options

1. Repeat the activity for several rounds with different sets of noun phrase cards.
2. Use the exercise as a quick review while forming groups for an upcoming activity.

Contributor

Nikki L. Ashcraft is a student in the TESL MS program at George State University, Atlanta, Georgia, and has served as a teaching assistant in the Cobb County Adult Education ESL program in Smyrna, Georgia, in the United States.

Empty Your Pockets

Levels
Beginning–intermediate

Aims
Practice the concepts of count and noncount, time frame, purpose

Class Time
Varies

Preparation Time
30 minutes or less

Resources
Everyday pocket/purse items

This activity improves the skills of identification, description, and comparison using the everyday objects that students carry with them.

Procedure

1. Seat students in a circle.
2. Ask all students to empty their pockets or purses on their desks (students may exclude any embarrassing items).
3. Call on students in any predetermined order to do one or more of the following:

   a. Give the name of each object: *This is* _____, *This is a/an* _____.
   b. Describe each object: color, size, texture, shape, value.
   c. Compare each object to similar objects: for example, *bigger than most, more expensive than* _____, *the heaviest.*
   d. Group students on the basis of the items: for example, *both* _____ *and, neither* _____ *nor, too, so, either.*
   e. Tell what each item is used for: for example, *I use this to/for (e.g., smoking, hair, writing).*
   f. Tell about the last time the item was used: past tense.
   g. Use other time frames: for example, *next time, how long, how often.*
   h. Discuss what can be guessed about each student from the items: for example, *maybe, may, I think, probably, must* (e.g., about country, interests, lives alone, lives on/off campus).

Caveats and Options

1. Pair students, with each student doing a, b, c, e, h for partner's items.
2. Put contents of pockets or purses into a paper bag (or use envelopes if bags aren't available) in such a way that no one else can see what is inserted.

4

    a. Have one student reach in and guess the contents of the bag from touch alone: saying, for example, *I think, I don't know, maybe.*

    b. Have another student reach in and describe what he or she feels: for example, *smooth, rough, soft, hard, flat, curved, heavy, metal, plastic, glass, fabric.*

Steps a and b can be combined by guessing what is recognized and describing what is not recognized.

3. The class guesses the use of unfamiliar objects: for example, *for, to.*
4. The class tries to guess who these things belong to: for example, *It's (Juan's), It belongs to* _____.
5. Without naming a particular student, the class tries to analyze what kind of person would carry these things: for example, *a person who* _____.
6. Empty your pocket or purse, either onto the desk or into a bag. Students do some of the activities suggested above—for example, with the vocabulary below, they form questions or statements about athletics, hobbies, pets, country: *small flashlight, emery board, checkbook, coin purse, tissues, barrette, pen knife, ballpoint pen, pills, chalk, peds, thimble, keys, pins, license, donor card, air mail stamps, band aid, library card, sweetener, candy or gum, medical card, credit cards, bank cards, fob on key chain.*
7. This activity probably can be used only once with each group. The alternatives chosen will depend on which grammatical pattern the teacher wants to reinforce.

Contributor

Margaret Fenimore Petty is the Intensive Program Coordinator in the English Language Programs at the University of Pennsylvania, in the United States.

Color Stories

Levels
High beginning +

Aims
Produce a variety of
adjectives in noun
phrases while practicing
word order

Class Time
25 minutes

Preparation Time
None

Resources
None

Students transform stories by adding color words or making other kinds of creative changes.

Procedure

1. Pair off students.
2. Select one student for demonstration.
3. Face the student so that the rest of the class can see and hear both of you.
4. Ask the student to tell you a short story (3–5 sentences). Listen carefully and maintain eye contact.
5. Tell the story back to the student, adding color adjectives to each noun phrase. For example:

Student: I bought a car yesterday. I drove to my house. Then I put my shirt and pants in my suitcase. I put the suitcase in the car and drove to the mountains.

Teacher: I bought a *red* car yesterday. I drove to my *blue* house. Then I put my *black* shirt and *white* pants in my *brown* suitcase. I put the *brown* suitcase in the *red* car and drove to the *green* mountains.

Ask the student if you repeated the story accurately.

6. Repeat the process, with you telling the story and the student repeating it. Emphasize that the repetition must use the same words as the original with the addition of the color words. Note that the colors do not have to be logical (i.e., you could have driven to the *pink* mountains).

7. Make sure that students understand the process, then let them tell stories on their own in pairs. Move around to different pairs and remind them to listen, concentrate, and repeat accurately.

Caveats and Options

1. Insert an adverb for each verb.
2. Use different types of adjectives (e.g., texture, smell, size, shape).
3. Trade partners after one round of stories.
4. Build the story round-robin style, with each student giving one sentence followed by the repetition with adjectives.
5. Ask groups of three or four students to add a series of adjectives to each noun.
6. This activity is a good, quick review of types of adjectives and adjective or adverb placement. It also enhances listening, concentration, and memory skills. The exercise was originally designed to help actors listen to each other and focus on exact wording.
7. Spolin (1963) stresses the need for eye contact between the members of the pair to help concentration. She also emphasizes that the listener should visualize the scene in color as the speaker tells it rather than try to add the colors afterwards.

References and Further Reading

Spolin, V. (1963). *Relating an incident. Improvisation for the theater: A handbook of teaching and directing techniques.* Evanston, IL: Northwestern University Press.

Contributor

Marianne Phinney is a CALL expert with InfoSoft International, Boston, Massachusetts, in the United States.

Puzzling Out Comparatives and Superlatives

Levels
Intermediate

Aims
Practice comparatives
and superlatives while
building vocabulary

Class Time
45 minutes

Preparation Time
Varies

Resources
Puzzles (see
Appendices)

A crossword puzzle creates a stimulating problem-solving environment for practicing comparative and superlative forms of adjectives and adverbs.

Procedure

1. Draw three circles and three rectangles of different sizes on the chalkboard, and label them 1, 2, and 3. The circles and rectangles on the board should be drawn with overlapping to simulate *farther* and *closer* objects, as in:

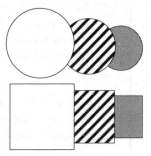

2. Use these objects to illustrate one object as *closer/farther* than another, and one as the *farthest/closest* one.
3. Point out to students that comparatives and superlatives are derived from adjectives or adverbs. Single syllable comparatives (e.g., *fast*) end in *-er* (*faster*), while words of two or more syllables (e.g., *important*) remain the same and may be preceded by the word *more* (*more important*). Also point out that single syllable superlatives (e.g., *fast*) end in *-est* (fastest), while words of two or more syllables (*important*) remain the same and are preceded by the words *the* and *most* (*the most important*).

8

4. After a brief explanation, and before giving out the puzzle, call on students individually to use comparatives and superlatives to compare the circles and boxes on the chalk board.
5. Give the students the clues and the puzzle to work on in pairs—one set per pair—to ensure that they will need to work together to solve it.
6. Check the students' productions orally or on an overhead transparency.

Caveats and Options

This exercise makes use of the four language skills. It calls for the student to listen to the explanation of comparatives and superlatives. It gives them an opportunity to communicate orally when working on the crossword puzzle and also to practice reading and writing to finish the task.

Appendix A: A Crossword Puzzle Using *-est, most*

SUPERLATIVES

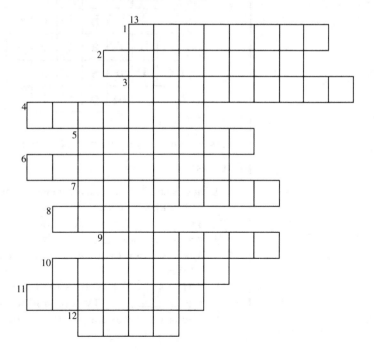

SUPERLATIVES

	13							
1	s	m	a	l	l	e	s	t

2 f u n n i e s t

3 p r e t t i e s t

4 t a l l e s t

5 l a r g e s t

6 s i m p l e s t

7 h e a v i e s t

8 m o s t

9 b i g g e s t

10 b r a v e s t

11 c l o s e s t

12 m o s t

Instructions: Fill in the blanks with a superlative.

Clues

1. Sue is smaller than anyone else in the class. She is the _____ of her classmates.
2. Yuko is very funny. She is the _____ girl in our class.
3. pretty, prettier, _____
4. Mike is taller than his brothers. He is the _____ one of all three.
5. Larry's hotel has a 25-foot TV screen. It is very large. It is the _____ TV screen in town.
6. The last test was simple. It was the _____ test this year.

7. Sam, the wrestler, weighs more than anyone else on the team. He is very heavy. Sam is the _____ wrestler on the team.
8. This is the _____ important test I will ever have to take.
9. Juan is big. Mike is bigger, but Al is the _____ of all.
10. brave, braver, _____
11. close, closer, _____
12. Washington State is the _____ beautiful state in the United States.
13. When we add *-est* to adjectives, they are called _____.

**Appendix B:
A Crossword
Puzzle Using
*-er, more***

COMPARATIVES

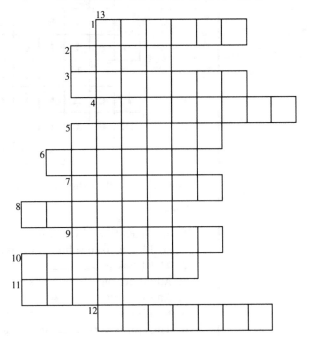

COMPARATIVES

¹c	l	o	s	e	r		
²m	o	r	e				
³s	m	a	l	l	e	r	
⁴p	r	e	t	t	i	e	r
⁵t	a	l	l	e	r		
⁶l	a	r	g	e	r		
⁷f	a	s	t	e	r		
⁸b	e	t	t	e	r		
⁹b	i	g	g	e	r		
¹⁰h	e	a	v	i	e	r	
¹¹m	o	r	e				
¹²s	m	a	r	t	e	r	

Instructions: Fill in the blanks with comparatives.

Clues

1. Sue lives three blocks from school. She lives very close. Jane lives six blocks from school. Sue lives _____ to school than Jane.
2. This book is _____ important than that book.
3. Adults are big. Babies are small. Babies are _____ than adults.
4. Ann is pretty, but Mary is much _____.
5. Kim is 6 feet tall. Kiyo is 5 feet tall. Kim is _____ than Kiyo.
6. The sun is very large. It is much _____ than the earth.
7. Emad can run one mile in 7 minutes. He can run very fast. Ali can run a mile in 6 minutes. Ali can run _____ than Emad.
8. good, _____, best

9. My home is small. Your home is big. Your home is _____ than mine.
10. Gold is very heavy. Aluminum is very light. Gold is _____ than aluminum.
11. My watch was _____ expensive than that one.
12. Terrence got an A on the exam. Lee got a C. Maybe Terrence is _____ than Lee.
13. When we add *-er* to adjectives, they are called _____.

Contributor

Larry J. Sinnott is Lecturer at Asia University's English Language Education Research Institute in Tokyo, Japan.

Adjective Order With Buttons

Levels
Beginning–intermediate

Aims
Practice adjective order using simple objects for visual contrast

Class Time
10–20 minutes

Preparation Time
10–15 minutes

Resources
Box of buttons

Caveats and Options

Buttons provide a concrete visual and kinesthetic model for working on adjectives.

Procedure

1. Choose buttons with clearly different sizes, shapes, and colors.
2. Orally model vocabulary by word groups, such as color (e.g., *red, white, yellow*), shape (e.g., *round, square*), and numbers. For example, hold up one button and say, "One blue button," and then hold up two and say, "Two blue buttons." Be careful to have only one contrast at a time. For example, do not contrast *one blue button* with *two red buttons* until you are sure the students know the individual words.
3. Ask students to take one or more buttons that you specify until they have demonstrated comprehension.
4. Have students ask each other for particular buttons. You will be monitoring for -*s* plural and adjective order, that is, *one blue button* not **one button blue.*

1. Any set of small, easily differentiated objects can be used instead of buttons.
2. This exercise might be thought of as "Silent Way Revisited." In the Silent Way method, small colored wooden rods are used to represent anything from number and color to prepositions, pronouns, nouns, and verbs. Although the rods have been praised for their flexibility, some students are uncomfortable with the rods because they seem too abstract. However, the same techniques of inducing vocabulary

and grammar from examples and then practicing them can be used with suitable real objects.

Contributor

Lise Winer is Associate Professor in the Department of Linguistics, Southern Illinois University, Carbondale, in the United States.

◆ Articles

Determiner Story

Levels
Intermediate +

Aims
Review the main grammatical conditions for use of *a, an,* and *the*
Review the spoken context for the use of the articles and attend to their appearance in writing

Class Time
Two 30-minute periods

Preparation Time
30 minutes

Resources
Any print source with good font variety (see Appendix)

Caveats and Options

Students learn to focus on the definite and indefinite articles through pasted up texts using different fonts.

Procedure

1. Assemble a short conversational text with many instances of English articles *a/an/the* in a variety of uses. For each article, use a font that differs in size and design from the previous one.
2. Read and discuss this demonstration passage with students, noting the different meanings of the article according to whether it classifies (e.g., *a river*) or identifies (e.g., *the Ohio*).
3. Include some instances of zero forms as well, such as plurals (e.g., *[0]students were joking*) and sometimes proper nouns (e.g., *[0] Ohio is my home*). The irregular fonts are a device to call the frequency or pattern of use to the students' attention. Also, the odd fonts, by exaggerating the appearance of the articles in the text, might call attention to the way they contribute to the rhythmic patterns of English.
4. Assign a subsequent day on which the student or students as a group submit a short conversational piece composed in the same way, by pasting in words from newsprint or old magazines. That day, have some or all of the students present and read their compositions for class discussion.

You may wish to ask the students to do one of a number of follow-up exercises, from rewriting some of the stories, to tackling tougher discourse (such as a section of the college catalogue), to compiling their own handbook of determiner samples, starting with the ones gathered for this exercise and adding others weekly. For example:

Determiners with noncount nouns:

the water
the money

Determiners with proper names:

the Washington Monument
the Potomac

or

[0] Pennsylvania
[0] Burger King

**Appendix:
Sample Text**

ON **The** ROAD

Marie: What is **the** matter?

Allan: I think that one of **the** tires is going flat.

Marie: Do you think that we can drive to **a** garage?

Allan: It's no use. We don't have *a* spare tire.

Marie: What happened to *the* spare?

Allan: I left it in town at *an* Exxon station and
have not gone back to get it.

Marie: Then stop at **the** next emergency telephone and I
will make **a** call to my brother. He can go to
Exxon station and pick up *the* spare tire.

Contributor

Harold Ackerman is Assistant Professor in the Department of Developmental Instruction at Bloomsburg University, Pennsylvania, in the United States.

Article Recipe

Levels
Intermediate +

Aims
Increase comprehension
of the article system
while developing the
ability to self-analyze
language production
Practice oral
communication in
English

Class Time
30–45 minutes

Preparation Time
10–15 minutes

Resources
Handouts (see
Appendices)

References and Further Reading

Thⁱs activity practices article choice in a series of interesting activities.

Procedure

1. Make copies of the recipe handout, any sports column, and the article choice chart.
2. Distribute the recipe, and read the story to the class. Discuss the reasons for the article choices.
3. Distribute the sports column. Have students complete the exercise individually and discuss the exercise answers in pairs.
4. Distribute the article choice chart and have students analyze errors in pairs.

Caveats and Options

1. The error analysis can be done as a homework assignment. Steps 3–7 may be repeated with different article choice exercises.
2. This is a supplement to a comprehensive explanation of the article system. The category *generic* is not included in Chart 1.

Celce-Murcia, M., & Larsen-Freeman, D. (1983). *The grammar book: An ESL/EFL teacher's course*. Cambridge, MA: Newbury House.

Appendix A: The Recipe Handout

Once I was walking in a jungle,
and I saw *a tiger*. *(indefinite singular count noun)*
I chased *the tiger*. *(definite singular count noun)*
I chased it into a jungle clearing
full of *tigers*. *(indefinite plural count noun)*
I looked at *the tigers* *(definite plural count noun)*
in surprise, and they looked at me
in anticipation. *Some tigers* *(indefinite plural count noun)*
started to chase me. When they
caught me, one tiger said that
I obviously wasn't sweet enough,
and he needed *some sugar*. *(indefinite noncount noun)*
They all agreed *sugar* *(generic noncount noun)*
was a crucial ingredient—
in fact, the most important ingredient—
in the recipe for _____ [Insert name].
Finally, they decided they couldn't
have me for *lunch because no one
had brought *the sugar*. *(definite noncount noun)*
(*Sugar* is bad for your teeth *(generic noncount noun)*
anyway.) So I lived to tell this story.

*"Lunch" is used as a synonym for *food* in this sentence and has a non-count meaning.

Appendix B: Review of Grammar Terms Handout

A count noun has both singular and plural forms: *tiger, tigers*.

A singular count noun requires *a, an*, or *the*. A plural count noun is accompanied by *the, some* or 0.

A noncount or mass noun does not have a singular or a plural form: for example, *sugar*.

A noncount noun is accompanied by *the, some*, or 0.

A general statement about a class or category expresses generic meaning:

> *Tigers* eat meat.
> *A tiger* is a meat-eating animal.
> *The tiger* is a meat-eating animal.

The tiger, a meat-eating animal, is very beautiful.
Sugar is bad for your teeth.

A noun that has been clearly identified by a specific description, previous reference, or setting expresses a definite meaning.

A noun that has not been clearly identified by a specific description, previous reference, or setting expresses an indefinite meaning.

Appendix C: Article Choice Charts

What types of nouns are causing you confusion? Use Charts 1 and 2 to help you choose the correct article.

Chart 1: Noun Types and Article Choices

	Common			Proper	
	Count		Noncount		
	Singular	Plural		Singular	Plural
Definite	the	the	the	0	the
Indefinite	a/an	some/0	some/0		

Chart 2

Noun	Noun Type	Article Choice

From Celce-Murcia & Larsen-Freeman (1983), p.172.
Used with permission.

Contributor

Michele H. Kilgore is in the doctoral program in speech communication at the University of Georgia, Athens, in the United States.

Article Rods

Levels
Beginning

Aims
Learn the basic function
of articles through
interactive discourse

Class Time
10–15 minutes

Preparation Time
5 minutes

Resources
Cuisenaire rods

Students practice the use of articles with cuisenaire rods.

Procedure

1. Prepare for the demonstration by placing a number of rods in plain view of the learners, making sure that for some of the colors, only one rod is present, while for others more than one is present. For example, using three red rods, four green rods, two orange rods, and a yellow rod, direct a volunteer in the following way:

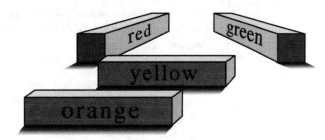

Teacher: Pick up a red rod.
         (There are three red rods)
Student: [Picks up the rod]
Teacher: Pick up the green rod.

Notice that the student cannot carry out this last command: The use of *the* asks the students to pick up a specific green rod, but it is not clear which green rod is being referred to.

2. Once students realize that they need to know which one to carry out the command, Pick up the green rod, they often respond by asking "Which one?" Sometimes, however, it is necessary to cue them.

21

Student: Which one?
Teacher: [Points] That one.
Student: [Does it]
Teacher: Pick up the yellow one. (There is only one yellow rod)

The command *Pick up a green rod* is, in contrast, no problem for the students.

Caveats and Options

1. As an alternative or follow-up, the following sequence may be used:

   Teacher: Pick up the orange rod. (There are two)
   Student: Which one?
   Teacher: [Points] That one.
   Student: [Does it]
   Teacher: Pick up a green rod and give it to the student.
   Student: Which student? (or Which one?)

   This final version, with its distinction between *a* student and *the* student, sometimes works well as a continuation, because the difference between *a* student and *the* student is more important to them than the earlier difference between *a* rod and *the* rod.

2. Follow-up listening exercises: The articles are difficult to hear because they are not only often phonologically unstressed but also reduced. An easy-to-make listening exercise can help with this. Simply record a short passage, omitting 8 or 10 of the articles, and then distribute copy of the article-less passage to the students. Their task is to fill in the missing articles. It may even be helpful to tell them how many are missing. Incidentally, other than saving your voice, an advantage of the tape recorder is that you cannot be accused of saying it differently each time it is read. Expect to have to do at least four or five repetitions of a passage before all the students can hear the articles, even when, to your ear the articles are clearly audible.

Contributor

Graham Thurgood is Professor of Linguistics at California State University, Fresno, in the United States.

◆ Subject-Verb Agreement Matchmaking

Levels
Beginning +

Aims
Recognize the structure of a sentence to identify the subject and predicate in complex sentences

Class Time
30–45 minutes

Preparation Time
10–15 minutes

Resources
Cardboard squares
Enough sentences (e.g., if there are 20 students in the class you should prepare 10 sentences)

Students work on subject-predicate coherence and subject-verb agreement by matching parts of sentences.

Procedure

1. Prepare 10 sentences. The degree of complexity depends on the level of the students.

Some suggested sentences (best in capital letters):

> DUCKS QUACK.
> THE BOY CRIES/IS CRYING.
> THE GIRLS LAUGH HAPPILY.
> MY MOTHER WATERED THE PLANTS.
> THE ONE STANDING IN THE DOORWAY IS MY BROTHER.
> OVEREXPLOITATION OF TROPICAL RAIN FORESTS WILL LEAD TO DEFORESTATION.
> THAT GONERIL HAD A SUPERNUMERARY EYE HAS NEVER BEEN NOTICED BY THE CRITICS.
> THE FACT THAT YOU RECEIVED NO BIRTHDAY GREETINGS FROM MARS DOESN'T MEAN THAT THE RED PLANET IS UNINHABITED.
> WHAT HAD IRRITATED HIM WAS THAT HE WAS NOT THE CAPTAIN.
> (Burton-Roberts, 1989)

2. Separate all the noun phrases (subject) from the verb phrases (predicate) and write each phrase on a cardboard square.
3. Have students do the following:
   - take one square and form a circle, holding their cardboard square in front of them
   - read aloud the phrase on their cardboard square

- move around and try to find their other half
- pair themselves up if they think they belong to a correct (both semantically and syntactically) sentence
- judge the sentences themselves

Caveats and Options

This activity is suitable for students of all levels by varying the difficulty and complexity of the sentences.

References and Further Reading

Burton-Roberts, N. (1989). *Analysing sentences: An introduction to English syntax.* New York: Longman.

Contributor

Eunice Tang is University Assistant Lecturer in the Department of English, City Polytechnic of Hong Kong.

Part II: Relative Clauses

Combining Information in Authentic Texts

Levels
Any

Aims
Choose correct/
acceptable relative
clause markers
Learn mechanics of
connecting sentences
using relative clauses
markers to place new
information in simple
sentences

Class Time
10–30 minutes

Preparation Time
10–30 minutes

Resources
Student writing, teacher
writing, authentic
materials from texts,
newspapers

With their own writing, students learn to use relative clauses or appositives to combine sentences.

Procedure

1. Obtain/make/write paragraphs with short sentences (6-10 words) that can be joined. The sentences should be in paragraphs that juxtapose short and long sentences (10-15 words) that cannot be joined because of lack of cohesion, or long sentences that should not be joined for stylistic reasons. Paragraphs are best if they are from 7-13 sentences long to ensure close reading and group discussion.
2. Leave space for the newly combined sentences below the readings. Depending on student level, you might want to write relative clause markers (or appositives) in parentheses at the end of the paragraph.
3. Do one example as a group on an overhead projection or the chalkboard to explain the mechanics of finding appropriate sentences, deciding how to combine them, and producing newly combined sentences in the place provided. Do not just make insertions with symbols; write the full sentence.
4. Create working groups of two or three students.
5. Give each member of the pair/group a copy of the paragraph(s).
6. Allow silence while each person reads the text(s).
7. As soon as a group arrives at a consensus as to which sentences can be joined and how, they can write their joined sentences in the space provided.
8. Put the students in new groups to check the correctness/appropriateness of the newly written sentences.

Caveats and Options

1. Repeat the activity more than once, first doing relative clauses, then appositives.
2. Vary the combining options using relative clauses, coordinators, subordinators, and other connectors.
3. This activity is best used to practice previously learned mechanics and to sensitize students to the conditions for relative clauses. It also sensitizes students to the use and misuse of relative clauses when adjectives of color, description, and prepositional phrases would be more appropriately used.

Appendix: Sample Exercises

Directions for Paragraph 1: Combine sentences in the following paragraph. Decide which sentences you can combine using the words in parentheses after the paragraphs. Finally, rewrite the sentences in the lines provided below the paragraph.

1. Valley View Tower has seven stories and is a woman's dormitory. The second through sixth floor rooms are all similar. They are all for undergraduate students. The seventh floor is very clean. It was remodelled recently. It is the quietest area in the dormitory.
(which)   (which)

_____

_____

_____

Directions for Paragraphs 2 and 3: Combine the sentences in the following paragraphs using relative clauses and/or appositives. Rewrite the sentences in the lines provided below the paragraphs. Be ready to give reasons for why you combined them or why you didn't combine other sentences.

2. A microcomputer lab is located on the second floor in the student center near Carousel Square. The lab has two long glass windows. The two glass windows extend from the ceiling to the floor. Also, it has a huge brown wooden door. The door has a dirty window. Inside, there are many paintings on the blue walls. Most of the paintings are of Utah.

_____

_____

_____

3. The Junction opens at five-thirty for dinner. Students come there to have dinner. Those students live in nearby residence halls. After they show their ID card, they can enter and stand in food lines. The menu is for oriental food, a salad bar, and microwaved potatoes. The menu changes every other day. Also, students can get four kinds of drinks there. It is usually a crowded and noisy place.

_____

_____

_____

The above three texts are useful with low intermediate to intermediate students.

Contributor

James E. Bame is Senior Lecturer in the Intensive English Language Institute of Utah State University, in the United States.

Definitions Game

Levels
High intermediate

Aims
Promote cognitive
understanding of clause
patterns
Build students'
awareness of a typical
pattern used in scientific
writing

Class Time
40–45 minutes

Preparation Time
1 hour

Resources
25 sets of matching
main clauses and
relative clause
definitions

In the format of a rummy card game, students match relative clauses to main clauses to make definitions.

Procedure

1. Create a set of cards for each group of students using strips of cardboard or index cards cut in half. Write (or paste a copy of) the main clause on one card and the matching relative clause definition on another. (Using different colors for main cards and adjective clause cards makes sorting easier when you put the game away.) Place each set of cards in a large envelope with directions pasted on the cover.

2. Explain to students how a rummy card game is played, demonstrating with three students before the whole class breaks into groups. (See the following steps for rummy directions if you are unfamiliar with the game.)

3. Place the students in groups of three so that all students can see everyone's hand of cards.

4. One student will distribute four main clause cards to each player in the group. These are placed face up so that everyone can see them. The remaining main clauses and the relative clauses are placed in two stacks, face down so that everyone in the group can reach them.

5. The next student then begins play by drawing a relative clause card from the stack. If a match can be made, the player keeps that card, putting it next to the matched main clause. Everyone in the group must agree that a good sentence has been made.

6. Once agreement is reached, the player draws a new main clause to replace the one that has been matched, and the next player tries his/her luck with the relative clause stack.

7. If a match cannot be made, the player puts the rejected relative clause on the table, face up, as part of a discard list. The next player, or later players, may choose from either the discard list or from the face down stack.
8. The winner of the game is the player with the most completed sentences at the end of the class, or when time up is called.

Caveats and Options

1. You may ask students to write down all of the completed sentences from their group so that you can check them later.
2. Students may create their own game cards, each student locating definitional relative clauses in their reading.
3. Although only a few sentences may actually be completed during the 40-minute session, the discussion of whether the relative clause fits seems to be a key to students' understanding of this structure.

Contributor

Elizabeth Hanson-Smith is Coordinator of the TESOL Program at California State University, Sacramento, in the United States.

Give Me the Book That's Mine

Levels
Intermediate +

Aims
Elicit a variety of
sentences in the
grammatical form of
relative clauses while
stimulating participation
through involvement of
personal property and
forced awareness of
details

Class Time
20–25 minutes

Preparation Time
None

Resources
Objects students have
on hand

In an activity based on objects they all possess, students learn to distinguish individual items using relative clauses.

Procedure

1. Decide on five very specific items (e.g., *ring* not *jewelry*) that you are sure every member of the class has in class.

   Suggested items:

textbook	notebook
pen	watch
pencil	school ID
piece of paper	

2. Write the five items on the board, making sure that each student has one of each. (You can always have a few extras of your own to pass out if needed.)
3. Tell the class to put their five items in front of them on their desks and to examine each one carefully for identifying marks and characteristics.
4. Create groups of six or seven students seated in a circle.
5. Have each group select a leader for the first round of the activity. Leadership will rotate with each item (e.g., five items—five leaders).
6. Start with the first item listed on the board—the textbook, for example. Each member of the group puts his or her book in front of the leader.
7. Going around the circle within each group, each student asks the leader to return his/her book by describing it using a relative clause. Give a pattern for the students to follow, writing it on the board and leaving it there for at least two rounds of the activity.

Suggested models:

Give me the book which (that) has a torn cover.
My book is the one which (that) . . . .

8. If the sentence is correct, the leader returns the book to the student who has made the request. If not, the student must correct the statement with the help of the other group members. The student may need help from groupmates on vocabulary as well as form (e.g., *torn, bent, cover*) before getting the book back.
9. Before letting the groups go off on their own, model the task in front of the whole class, choosing five dependable students to give you their books and to ask for them back using the pattern.
10. Have groups go through this activity with all five items, rotating leaders for each round of the activity.

Caveats and Options

1. To better monitor student performance, check for accuracy as a whole-class activity (if the class is small enough).
2. A more advanced class can handle more variety in the model sentences.
3. The same activity can be used for prepositional phrases (e.g., *with the torn cover, on the top of the pile, to the left of the green pencil*), which are reduced relative clauses.

Contributor

Victoria Holder teaches ESL at San Francisco State University and San Francisco City College, in California, in the United States.

Identity Game

Levels
Intermediate

Aims
Practice restrictive
relative clauses and yes/
no questions in a game
format
Promote group spirit
and enthusiasm

Class Time
30 minutes

Preparation Time
None

Resources
None

Teams try to guess the identity of a well-known person or thing by forming yes/no questions with restrictive relative clauses.

Procedure

1. Divide the students into two teams, each sitting on opposite sides of the classroom. Ask each team to choose its own name. Write the team names on the board.
2. Explain the activity to the class.
3. Call on one student from Team A to come to the front of the class. He or she is to think of a well-known person or thing and whisper it to the teacher.
4. Begin by calling on someone from Team B. He must ask a yes/no question containing a restrictive relative clause to try to guess the person's or thing's identity. For example, *Is this someone who speaks English? Is this something that is living?*
5. Then call on someone from Team A. Alternate turns from team to team until a certain number of questions have been asked (12 seems to work well). Keep track of how many questions have been asked.
6. Instead of asking a question when it's his or her turn, a student may guess the identity of the person/thing. If correct, his orher team is awarded three points. (Keep track of the points on the board.) If incorrect, the team loses a point. Note that cheating, blurting out the answer out of turn, or repeating someone else's question, also results in a loss of one point.
7. When the person/thing has been identified, call a new person up to the front of the class from Team B. If no one has guessed the identity by the designated number of questions, call the game a draw and supply the answer.

8. If the class is small, play continues until everyone has had a chance at the front of the class. If it is a large class, play a designated number of rounds and then tally up the score. The team with the most points wins.

Contributor

Tracy M. Mannon teaches English at the University of Neuchâtel, Switzerland.

Who Is It?

Levels
Intermediate +

Aims
Distinguish between
restrictive and
nonrestrictive relative
clauses
Learn to set off
nonrestrictive relative
clauses with commas

Class Time
25 minutes

Preparation Time
None

Resources
Overhead projector
(OHP), chalkboard, or
whiteboard

This activity offers a functional way to highlight the differences between restrictive and nonrestrictive relative clauses using contrasting who-clauses to describe class members.

Procedure

1. Ask three or four different students what country they are from. Then ask if they know where you are from. In my case, at least some of them know that I am from Canada.
2. Put the following sentences on the board:

   Point to the student *who is from Ethiopia.*
   Point to the student *who is from Malaysia.*
   Point to the student *who is from Mexico.*
   Point to the teacher, *who is from Canada.*

It is quickly apparent that, to obey the first three commands, the information in the relative clause helps answer the question, Which one?, but not for the fourth. Make sure that the students notice that if the relative clauses in the first three examples are erased, we do not know which student is being referred to; if the relative clause in the last example is erased, they can still point to the teacher. In writing, the difference between restrictive and nonrestrictive relative clauses is indicated by the punctuation. Restrictive relative clauses are not punctuated; nonrestrictive relative clauses are set off from the rest of the sentence by commas.

Caveats and Options

1. Further examples of a parallel kind can be made up about the classroom, about the students, or about anything they all know. The only crucial requirement is that the examples be real in the same way that the examples given in this text were real for my own class.

2. The difference between restrictive and nonrestrictive relative clauses is relatively easy to illustrate, but much harder to explain. For many students, this simple demonstration is quite useful.

Contributor

Graham Thurgood is Professor of Linguistics at California State University, Fresno, in the United States.

Part III: Tenses

♦ Present Tense Transformation Chart

Levels
Low intermediate

Aims
Make statements and
questions using simple
present tense
Use temporal
expressions and
frequency adverbs
appropriately

Class Time
30–45 minutes

Preparation Time
3 minutes

Resources
Chalkboard or overhead
projector

Students describe their own habitual activities and then ask other students about their activities, using the simple present tense and adverbial expressions from a chart.

Procedure

1. Create a five-line, five-column chart. The first column should be long enough to write a sentence, the three middle columns big enough to write in a name, and the fifth column sentence length. This chart may be drawn on the board or on an overhead transparency for students to copy.
2. Students number the lines 1–5. In the first column, they write five sentences about their daily habits. These sentences should be written in the first person. (e.g., *I go to church on Sunday.*)
3. The three middle columns are labeled *Sometimes*, *Always*, and *Never*. Students orally transform their five statements about themselves into questions to ask the other students. The students answering should respond by telling how frequently they do those same things.

   For example: Written Student 1: I go to church on Sunday.
   Oral   Student 1: Do you go to church on Sunday?
   Oral   Student 2: I never go to church on Sunday.

4. Upon hearing the responses to their questions, students write the name of the person they questioned in the block under the frequency adverb used in that person's response. (e.g., Student 1 will write Student 2's name under Never.) Students should question at least one other person about each of his or her five daily habits so that there will be at least one name under the frequency adverbs in each line.

41

More proficient and motivated students can attempt to fill in all of the blocks under the frequency adverbs by interviewing every student.

5. Using the names and the frequency adverbs as prompts, students write a statement in the fifth column about the students they interviewed. These statements should be in the third person. (e.g., *Marie never goes to church on Sunday.*)

6. Each student in the class reads one statement they wrote about another person.

Caveats and Options

1. If students need additional practice, a sixth column may be added to allow space for students to write the questions they will be asking their classmates. In the activity above, the chart is primarily a prompt.

2. When students begin to question each other, their discussions may become involved, especially when Student 1 always performs a certain act, and Student 2 never does.

Contributor

Nikki L. Ashcraft is a student in the TESL MA program at George State University, Atlanta, and has served as a teaching assistant in the Cobb County Adult Education ESL program in Smyrna, Georgia, in the United States.

What Are They Doing?

Levels
Beginning

Aims
Practice present
progressive in an
enjoyable way without
concentrating unduly on
form
Engage in discussion
while trying to guess
actions from drawings

Class Time
15–25 minutes

Preparation Time
2 minutes

Resources
5–15 sheets of old
paper/student
Colored pencils or
crayons

Students have fun creating pictures to illustrate present continuous actions and then guessing what actions are represented in each others' pictures.

Procedure

1. On the board, draw five large picture frames and then draw a stick person (or people) in each frame. Each of the people should be doing something specific, such as reading a book, painting a house, or playing tennis.
2. Model the question *What is he doing?* (or *she* or *they*, depending on your drawing). Elicit responses from the students until you hear the one that you had intended when you drew the picture. Continue until you have done all five frames. (When you hear an inappropriate response, say, for example, "No, he is not riding a horse" to provide input of the negative form.)
3. Now it is the students' turn. Give each student a set number of sheets (at least five) recycled paper or old paper used on only one side. Any size is fine, so you can have the students tear the paper in half if you like.
4. Give the students 5–10 minutes to complete their drawings. Encourage students to add objects or place settings for the verbs (e.g., a book for *He is reading*; spaghetti/restaurant for *She is eating*; a pool for *They are swimming*). This will allow you to expand this activity later. (See Caveats and Options below.)
5. Collect all of the drawings. Hold up a picture and gesture to elicit the appropriate question (e.g., *What is he doing?*, *What is she doing?*, or *What are they doing?*) and then the appropriate answer. Repeat this for three or four drawings.

6. If you have a small class, let students take turns being the teacher. If you have a large class, divide students into groups of four to six students. Give each group some of the drawings (the number of drawings times the number of students in the group). Students within each group should take turns being the teacher.

Caveats and Options

1. After students have given appropriate responses to all of the drawings, have students come up with three alternative answers. For example, if the correct response for a given drawing is *She's reading a book*, the students could also say *She's studying English, She's learning new words*, or *She is falling asleep*.
2. Practice information questions based on the drawings. For example, ask "What is she reading?" or "Where is she reading?" But be careful: Questions with *why* do not usually elicit the present progressive (e.g., *Why is she reading? Because she has a test tomorrow. Because she likes to read.*) In addition, *who* produces unnatural answers (e.g., *Who is reading? He is.* Because we can see this already, it produces an awkward response). Finally, *when* is also inappropriate because the present progressive signifies now or right now by definition.
3. The present progressive is not a difficult grammar point for most students. This exercise is an enjoyable way to practice this point because the students enjoy seeing (and laughing at) each other's art. In addition, it is a way to make use of old paper.
4. The drawings can be collected and used again for reviewing present progressive or for later practice on *going to* (e.g., *What's he going to do tomorrow? He's going to read a book.*)

Contributor

Keith S. Folse is the author of several ESL texts published by the University of Michigan Press.

Getting Students to Sit Down

Levels
Any

Aims
Produce and understand
descriptive statements
about appearance

Class Time
2–3 minutes/student

Preparation Time
5 minutes

Resources
None

This activity, adapted from the Total Physical Response technique, fosters production and comprehension of statements concerning appearance.

Procedure

1. Each student must think of five statements (three in the negative form) of the following types:

   These students have long hair/blue eyes/blond hair . . .
   These students are not wearing jeans/a skirt/a dress . . .
   These students usually wear a hat/glasses/a watch . . .
   These students are not tall.
   These students do not often wear ties/gloves/jewelry . . .

2. Ask all the students to stand and have one student come to the front and address the class. When he or she speaks, all students to whom the statement applies sit down. The aim is to have all the students who are still standing after four statements sit down after the fifth statement. Thus, for example:

   Student 1: These students have blond hair. All students with blond hair sit down.
   Student 2: These students usually wear glasses. All students who usually wear glasses sit down.
   Student 3: These students are not wearing a dress. All students not wearing dresses sit down.
   Student 4: These students are not more than 6 feet tall. All students 6 feet and under sit down.
   Student 5: These students do not have blue eyes. All students with eyes other than blue sit down.

Caveats and Options

1. The activity may be carried out as a whole class or in small groups. As negative questions pose the most difficulty, one can make the task more demanding by having students produce five negative statements. You need not restrict the activity to statements about appearance. It can easily be extended to hobbies, characteristics, or other subjects of interest to the class.

2. Ideally, this activity should be a spontaneous one obliging the student whose turn it is to think on his or her feet. However, if this is too demanding, you can allow students a period of written preparation although they should not be allowed to read their statements.

Contributor

Ronald Sheen teaches in the Faculty of Education at Tottori University, Tottori, Japan.

◆ Past Tense
The Party

Levels
Low intermediate

Aims
Preview or revisit the
past progressive with
while in creating a story

Class Time
10–15 minutes

Preparation Time
None

Resources
Chalkboard or overhead
projector (OHP)

This story taps into a learning strategy known as mnemonics. The idea is to make the story so memorable that students incorporate the basic structure into their repertoire. The story is developed around a particular structure—in this case, the past progressive with *while*—which is repeated many times as the story develops.

Procedure

1. Thank a particular student for the great party last night while drawing a two-story house with four rooms and a slanted roof on the board or overhead transparency.
2. Include all students in setting the scene: *Isn't the house beautiful? How did you like the food? . . .*

47

3. Draw two dancers in one room while asking which of your students they were. Write names volunteered by students next to the dancers.
4. In the next room, follow the same procedure with a grand piano. Draw one student at the piano and one student standing and listening. (e.g., *Was that Mozart?*)
5. Do the same for the next room, with three or four students sitting at a bar (e.g., *Who was that next to you, Yumi? What drink was that in his hand?*)
6. In the final room, draw a bed with one student sleeping. He is the party pooper. (Tell the host, e.g., *Don't invite Juan again!*)
7. Stress the time of the party: *When was this? Last night.* Help students make sentences with this model: *Yumi was drinking while Juan was sleeping.* (Another example: *While Kwan and Aysche were dancing, I was playing piano.*) Write *while* in the roof segment after a few sentences have been created.
8. After students contribute many sentences, elicit a summary concerning long (progressive, continuous) actions happening at the same time in the past.
9. Write (or have students write) sample sentences on the board or in their notebooks.
10. Assign a homework story that begins: *We had a wonderful time at the party last night.*

Caveats and Options

1. Have students generate sentences in groups.
2. Have student pairs alternate asking questions: *What were you doing while . . . ?*
3. Generate other stories on this model or have students generate stories around this grammatical structure.
4. Drawing ability is not necessary. Stick figures are fine.
5. These mnemonic stories usually work best as a follow-up review and reinforcement for the first few minutes of a class. But sometimes they can be tried to introduce a structure if the teacher has some confidence and if the class is motivated.

Acknowledgments

I thank my colleagues, Sue Lake, in particular, for the mnemonic story idea.

Contributor

Patricia Brenner, Teacher Educator and ESL Instructor at the University of Washington, is presently a Fulbright scholar at Bilkent University in Ankara, Turkey.

A Tense Situation

Levels
Intermediate

Aims
Create a variety of
questions and responses
using simple past and
past progressive tenses

Class Time
30–40 minutes

Preparation Time
10 minutes

Resources
Copies of a short
newspaper article on a
sensational crime

Students practice simple past and past progressive question-and-response patterns in the context of an incomplete story about a crime.

Procedure

1. Retype the article, leaving blank important pieces of information. Make a copy of the article for every student in the class.
2. On each copy, fill in one piece of missing information from the story so that every student has different information. For example, one student may have the time when a bank robbery occurred and another might have information on how much money was stolen.
3. Set the scene for the activity by asking students to imagine that a bank robbery has occurred. Elicit typical questions that the police might ask when called to the scene, such as *When did the robbery occur?, What did the robber look like?, What was s(he) wearing?*, and *What were you doing at the time of the robbery?*
4. Hand out the copies of the article to the students and explain that each has information about a different aspect of the crime. Their goal is to circulate among the other students asking questions until they are able to complete the whole story. The first student to do this wins the game.
5. Before the students circulate, have them practice forming possible questions to elicit information about the crime.
6. Have students circulate around the class asking questions and filling in the blanks. If they do not have the information when questioned by other students, they can just say, "I don't know," and move on to another student, being careful not to look at each others' sheets.
7. When one student feels that he or she has all the blanks completed, go through the story, checking the answers with the whole class.

Caveats and Options

1. This information gap activity allows students extensive oral practice in a communicative setting.
2. This activity is best used to practice simple past and past progressive question and response forms after students have a basic mastery of these tenses.

Contributor

Jane Dresser is Senior Instructor in ESL at Portland State University, Oregon, in the United States.

Who Did What?

Levels
Beginning–intermediate

Aims
Practice the past tense
in yes/no questions and
affirmative and negative
statements while
completing a task

Class Time
15–20 minutes

Preparation Time
5 minutes

Resources
Paper
Chalkboard

This exercise stimulates use of regular and irregular forms of the past tense in yes/no questions and affirmative and negative statements as by-products of a guessing game.

Procedure

1. On a sheet of paper, make two columns. In the left column, write the names of seven people (e.g., Maria, Kumio). In the right column, write seven actions in the past tense (e.g., *wrote a letter to the teacher, played tennis with some friends, studied English all day yesterday*). Then draw lines connecting each of the seven people to one of the seven actions. The result should be seven complete sentences that are grammatical and make sense. (Try to avoid *his/her/their* so as to limit clues and thereby make the activity more challenging.)
2. Write the two columns (people and actions) on the board. Do not draw the lines connecting the parts of the seven sentences.
3. Explain to the students that you have seven sentences of who did what and that they have to ask yes/no questions to guess which person did which action. (You may have to demonstrate by drawing a few lines to create sample sentences. Erase these before you begin the actual practice.)
4. In this group demonstration, divide the class into two or three groups that will compete to solve the mystery. In turn, have a student from each group ask you questions such as *Did Kumio write a letter to the teacher?* or *Did Maria watch television last night?* If the answer is yes, then another student in the same group can ask the next question. If the answer is no, the turn passes to a student in another group. When a student guesses the statement (the person and the action), that group is awarded 1 point. Because there are seven questions, a tie score is impossible.

Caveats and Options

1. In Steps 1-3, the students practice questions in the past tense but do not have to practice affirmative or negative statement forms. For maximum language practice (both in terms of volume of language and variety of forms, i.e., question, affirmative, and negative forms), have the students work in groups of three. Students will need to make up their own original lists, in two copies: one with the lines (i.e., the answers) drawn in and another which the other two students can look at while they are asking questions. If the activity is done in this manner, it triples the amount of the target grammar structure that students have to use.

2. This kind of problem-solving activity elicits a far greater amount of the target grammar structure in a natural and pleasant way than most traditional fill-in-the-blank grammar exercises ever do.

Contributor

Keith S. Folse is the author of several ESL texts published by the University of Michigan Press.

Around the World

Students move around the class as they form the past tense of irregular verbs.

Levels
Beginning–intermediate

Aims
Develop mastery of irregular verb forms with the visual and physical stimulation of a game

Class Time
15–20 minutes

Preparation Time
15 minutes

Resources
Large cards and a list of irregular verb forms

Procedure

1. Write the base form of irregular verbs on one side of a card, and write the past tense form (or past participle form) on the opposite side. Make approximately 20–50 cards (depending on time available and level).
2. Have students sit at desks. Have a student (or the teacher, at first) hold the cards and serve as leader of the activity.
3. Have one student move from his or her desk and stand next to a sitting student.
4. Have the leader reveal the first card in the stack showing the base form, for example, *eat*. The first student to correctly state the past tense form *ate* wins this round and then travels to the next seated student. Have the other student sit down.
5. In order to win, a student must travel ''around the world'' and back to his or her original desk.
6. Call a rematch for any simultaneous answers.

Caveats and Options

1. If the class comprises more than 20 students, divide the class to make two ''worlds.'' One of the students can display the cards to the second group.
2. This activity can be used to reinforce students' knowledge of irregular verb tense forms after they have been newly exposed to them. It is a useful and exciting game to help review these forms.

3. This activity can also be used in bilingual classrooms to practice vocabulary items. For example, a word in Spanish could be written on one side, with the English equivalent on the reverse.

Contributor

Cheri Ladd teaches at California State University, Fresno, and at the Fresno Adult School, in the United States. Thomas Nixon teaches in the American English Institute at California State University, Fresno, and is a candidate for the MA in Linguistics (TESL emphasis) at that university.

From Beginning to End

Levels
Intermediate +

Aims
Practice accurate use of
the past tense and other
linguistic features of
short narratives while
developing creative
storytelling skills

Class Time
1 hour

Preparation Time
10 minutes

Students practice the past tense and work on temporal connectors and other transition words by developing stories to connect a first and last sentence.

Procedure

1. Write a sentence (or several sentences) that could serve as the beginning of a story. For example, *It was a cold, wet Sunday in February. Georgina thought it would be a good day to stay at home and read a book.* Then write several possible endings for the story, preferably endings that are somewhat unexpected or intriguing, for example,

    a. When she came out of the wardrobe, it had disappeared.
    b. When she looked at herself in the mirror, she couldn't believe how much she had changed.
    c. After that, Georgina decided it was time to move.

Make enough endings for the story so that each group (See Step 2) can have a different one.

2. Divide the class into groups of three or four. If you have many groups in the class, some groups may use the same ending. Give each group a beginning and end of a story. Appoint one student in each group as a group scribe.
3. Ask each group to plan a story that fills in the missing information. Set a time limit, for example, 10–15 minutes.
4. As the groups work on their tasks, go around and give feedback as necessary.
5. Stop the activity after an appropriate time period (e.g., 15 minutes) so group scribes can tell their group's story.
6. Ask the class to discuss and then vote for the best story in their groups.

Caveats and Options

1. Students can write out their stories during class or for homework.
2. Give a list of specific lexical or other items which students must use in their story, for example:

jockey
helicopter
Inspector Poffis
but before doing that . . .
when she realized this . . .
the next thing she remembered was . . .

Contributor

Dino Mahoney is University Lecturer at the City Polytechnic of Hong Kong.

Recreating the Past Through Narrative Drama

Levels
Intermediate

Aims
Practice oral and written production of past tense forms in narratives

Class Time
30–40 minutes

Preparation Time
15 minutes

Resources
Adequate classroom space

Students reconstruct a past event based on mimed dramatizations.

Procedure

1. Arrange the classroom so that there is as much open space as possible for students to move around in. If possible, create an open space in the middle of the room by moving furniture against the walls of the classroom.
2. Tell your students that they are going to watch you mime the story of what happened to you on the bus yesterday. Also tell them that when you have finished, you will ask them to tell you what happened to you.
3. Mime the story:

   While you are on a crowded bus, someone steps on your toe, someone tries to steal your purse, the bus stops suddenly and you lurch to one side, you try to get off the bus but you cannot as the bus is so crowded, you step on someone's toe and apologize, you get off the bus at the following stop.

4. Elicit from the class what happened to you. Stress that this happened yesterday by beginning the elicitation with, "Okay, what happened to me yesterday? Where was I? What was I doing? What was the first thing that happened?"
5. Write the verbs on the board as the students give them to you:

   was riding
   stepped on
   tried to steal
   stopped

lurched
tried to get off
stepped on
apologized
got off

6. Using the verb list as a prompt, now tell the story of your bus journey to your students. You can add additional details, but keep the main events the same as in your mimed account.
7. Ask your students to pair off and tell each other the story of what happened to their teacher on the bus yesterday. Monitor them as they do this.
8. When they have finished, ask them, in pairs, to identify the irregular verbs in the list and to supply their present tense forms. Check their answers.
9. Now ask the students in pairs to think of a short anecdote about something that happened to them recently. Give them prompts on the board, for example, something that happened to you, (a) in a supermarket, (b) in class, (c) at home, (d) by the sea. Tell the students that they are free to make up imaginary events. Ask them to do this orally.
10. When the students have thought of a story, ask them to practice miming it.
11. Ask one pair of students to join up with another pair, each student selecting a partner from the other pair.
12. Ask students to mime their story to their partner in turn.
13. The original pairs get back together, separating from their new partners, and reconstruct the story that they saw mimed. Tell the students that all stories must begin, "Yesterday . . . "
14. The two pairs who worked together get back together once more and tell each other the stories that they saw mimed, confirming or correcting each others' interpretations as the narrative unfolds.
15. The student pairs write two short narratives of their own mimed account and the observed mimed account.

Caveats and Options

1. This activity can also be used at higher levels by making the mimed account more intricate.
2. Students can be given written narratives that they then have to turn into mime. The students mime, observe, and then reconstruct the mimed account into oral and written narratives. They then consult the written narratives and compare their own written versions with them.
3. This activity is an enjoyable way of reviewing past tense forms and involves creativity, imagination, and lots of participation by all students.

Contributor

Dino Mahoney is University Lecturer at the City Polytechnic of Hong Kong.

Communication Lines

Levels
Beginning–intermediate

Aims
Form questions and
responses in the past
tense in a communi-
cative context
Develop conversational
skills to begin, continue,
and end an interaction

Class Time
10 minutes

Preparation Time
5 minutes

Resources
None

Students in circles or lines question each other about their weekend activities to practice wh-questions and the past tense.

Procedure

1. Seat participants in two concentric circles or semicircles if space permits. If space does not permit or if seats are bolted down, have the first row turn and face the second, the third row face the fourth, and so on.
2. Explain to students that they are going to have a conversation using the past tense. Review greetings and leave takings. (e.g., *Hello. It's been nice talking to you. Goodbye.*)
3. Students on the outside or in the odd rows begin the conversation with the question, "What did you do last weekend?"
4. Students on the inside respond with a truthful answer.
5. Students on the outside ask several more questions, each about the content they have just heard.

For example:

Student 1: Hello, how are you?
Student 2: Fine, thank you, and you?
Student 1: OK. I tried to call you. What did you do last weekend?
Student 2: I went to the movies.
Student 1: What did you see?
Student 2: I saw *Gone with the Wind*.
Student 1: How did you like it?
Student 2: It was OK. I couldn't understand all of it. Some of the people speak funny.
Student 1: I know. I had the same problem.

61

Student 2: What did you do last weekend?
Student 1: I went to the disco.

6. At this point, Student 2 asks several questions following the same format.
7. After each student has asked several questions, they say goodbye and part company (5 minutes or less).
8. The inside row stands up and moves one seat to the right. The person on the end takes the first seat on the left if a semicircle or in rows.
9. The process begins again.
10. The teacher remains inside the circle or semicircle, but always behind the students so as to provide assistance when necessary.

Caveats and Options

1. Any past tense questions may be used.
2. Students choose the topic or grammar point they wish to practice.
3. If the group is large, keeping them in rows rather than circles is more manageable.
4. This activity is good as a warm-up or review. When used at the beginning of class, students arrive on time. When used at the end of class, they leave feeling stimulated. After using these lines several times, students become very adept at arranging their chairs very quickly.

Acknowledgments

Father Paul LaForge of Nanzan University originated this activity.

Contributor

Adelaide Heyde Parsons is Professor and ESOL Coordinator at Southeast Missouri State University, in the United States.

Square Dancing

Levels
Intermediate

Aims
Review the use of the past continuous tense and the simple past while learning the culture and music of U.S. square dancing

Class Time
Two 50-minute periods

Preparation Time
Varies

Resources
A recording of "Old Brass Wagon" or any children's game song, preferably without the words

Students learn square dancing as a context for actions which are then reviewed by contrasting the past progressive tense with the simple past.

Procedure

1. Introduce the music.
2. In TPR (Total Physical Response) fashion, teach a few simple maneuvers such as:

   Choose your partner.
   Circle to the right/left.
   Honor your partner/corner.
   Swing your partner/corner.
   Do-si-do.
   Promenade home.

3. When the students can follow the calls in time to the music, ask them to call out the directions in unison as they are doing the steps.
4. Next, let anyone who wants to act as the caller.
5. After the dance, give out contextual cues related to the square dance vocabulary.

   For example:

   What were you doing _____ ?
   a. in the circle
   b. with your partner
   c. as you were dancing back to back
   d. as you were moving around the circle

6. Encourage students in groups of three or four to create their own dialogue using questions such as:

What were you thinking about while you were dancing?
Were you thinking about the folk dances in your country?

Caveats and Options

If there are students who do not wish to participate in such an activity, ask them to be callers or reporters explaining the square dance to newcomers.

Contributor

Martha S. Stockstill tutors through her English teaching service, Real English, and teaches part-time for Hinds Community College in Jackson, Mississippi, in the United States.

You Are What You Eat

Levels
Beginning–intermediate

Aims
Practice asking
questions in the past
tense while learning
names of foods

Class Time
30–60 minutes

Preparation Time
30 minutes

Resources
Six Basic Foods Chart
(see Appendix)

The nature of a good diet is the focus of this activity, in which learners use and hear similar patterned sentences in the past tense over and over while they seek or transmit information.

Procedure

1. Give students copies of the Six Basic Foods Chart, briefly explaining what it is and the importance of a balanced diet.
2. Ask the students to write down what they had for lunch/breakfast/ dinner and the items in each food group. When students do not know how to say or spell a name of food, encourage them to ask you. Pronounce the item and write its the name on the board.
3. Ask the students to check each food item with the chart to see where it belongs. The students may ask: *Which group does _____ belong to?* Explain that taking foods from all six groups creates a well-balanced diet. Consuming foods from five different groups is acceptable, but if the food items cover fewer than four groups, the students should try to eat a greater variety of food.
4. After self-evaluation, each student reports the result of the evaluation to the class. For example, *I had some spaghetti, salad, and ice cream for dinner last night. According to the chart, I had food from only four different groups. My diet will be perfect if I add some food with protein such as fish, meat, and beans, and some green-yellow vegetables such as carrots and spinach.*
5. After the reports, make groups of about five students to have a discussion abut health and diet. The following are examples of topics:

   a. What did you find out and how did you feel about your own and your friends' diet?
   b. What is a perfect menu for breakfast/lunch/dinner, if you can eat whatever you like?

    c. What is a perfect menu for breakfast/lunch/dinner, if you consider your health and the chart?

    d. What does food mean to you?

Caveats and Options

1. This activity can be used as a role play by pairing students and assigning one of them the role of a dietitian. The dietitian asks questions such as: "What did you have for breakfast this morning?" The other student answers what he or she had and the dietitian evaluates the diet and gives the student some advice. The students take turns playing the dietitian.
2. Gatbonton and Segalowitz (1988) observed that automatized utterances resemble formulaic speech and argued that learners can develop automaticity by participating in communicative classroom activities that require repitition.

References and Further Reading

Gatbonton, E., & Segalowitz, N. (1988). Creative automatization: Principles for promoting fluency within a communicative framework. *TESOL Quarterly, 22*, 474–492.

Appendix: Six Basic Foods Chart

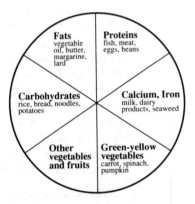

Contributor

Megumi Takeo, an EFL teacher in Chiba, Japan, is enrolled in the Temple University of Japan MA in TESOL program.

What's It All About?

Levels
Intermediate

Aims
Make informed guesses
and collect information
to complete an
explanation to a story,
using yes/no questions

Class Time
35–40 minutes

Preparation Time
15 minutes

Resources
Short story or anecdote
Deck of Bicycle brand
playing cards (optional)

This activity consolidates students' accurate use of yes/no questions and maximizes students' participation in class as they construct accurate yes/no questions to find the solution to a puzzle.

Procedure

1. Prepare a short suspense story or a short anecdote.
2. Tell the class the story, leaving out details that help explain the ending of the story. (e.g., *A man was found dead in his room. There were 53 bicycles all over the room.*)
3. Ask the students to repeat the facts of the story they have just heard. Check if they have retained the basic facts.
4. Divide the class into groups of three or four.
5. Give each group 5–10 minutes to discuss the story and to figure out the missing ideas in the most logical and sensible way.
6. For confirmation, have each group take turns asking the teacher one yes/no question about the story (e.g., *Was the man killed by the bicycles? Did he kill himself?*). The teacher should correct structural errors as necessary, and then answer the questions using only short responses (e.g., *No, he wasn't. No, he didn't.*)
7. (optional) After a few rounds of questions, the teacher may give a clue to help the students and give them some time for further discussion before proceeding.
8. The activity finishes when the first group completes the whole story in its original, logical sense.

Caveats and Options

1. If the class is small, the students can work together as one group and each of them takes turns asking one yes/no question until they get all the missing information regarding the story.

2. Depending on the students' proficiency level, a posted list of grammatical items such as *be, do* auxiliary, past, present, singular, and plural would assist the students in error correction.

Appendix: Sample Story

A possible suspense story that can be used for this activity follows:

The Story

A man was found dead in his room. There were 53 bicycles all over the room.

The Missing Ideas

The man was playing cards (these cards have a bicycle trademark) with some other people. He tried to cheat the others by using an extra card. Unfortunately, he was caught in the act and was subsequently shot to death. All 53 cards, including his extra card, were scattered around the room with the dead man.

Contributors

Matilda M. W. Wong is University Assistant Lecturer in the Department of English, City Polytechnic of Hong Kong, Hong Kong. Ken Fujioka is English Instructor at the Language Institute of Japan.

◆ Present Perfect Down and Out

Levels
Intermediate

Aims
Preview or revisit the present perfect with negatives, *for*, and *since*
Generate a grammatical structure from a picture prompt

Class Time
10–15 minutes

Preparation Time
None

Resources
Chalkboard or overhead projector (OHP)

The mnemonic story idea (see "The Party," p. 47) is used to elicit negative statements in the present perfect tense with *for* and *since*.

Procedure

1. Ask a particular student if you may tell the class about his or her brother. Ask the brother's name and begin to draw a picture of the brother, filling in the details as you speak. (Or put a completed picture on the OHP.)
2. Begin the story:

   Of course we all know that [student] is an excellent student, but unfortunately *John* (the brother) isn't studying. As you can see, he is really down on his luck. Now he lives in (*San Francisco*). Look at him! Tell me about his *fingernails* (*very long*), *hair* (*long and dirty*), *beard*, *clothes*, (*torn and dirty*), *no shoes*, *skinny* . . . Isn't this terrible.

   What about *cut his fingernails*? No? We want to talk about from the past up to the present. (Help students: *He hasn't cut his fingernails for 3 months.*)

3. Continue with negative + *for*: *bath* (*He hasn't taken a bath for a year.*); *change clothes*; *brush his teeth*; *have a good meal* . . . .
4. Now use *since* and build similar sentences.

Caveats and Options

1. Let the students do the creating, not you.
2. Use this story as a quick review or reinforcement or as a continuation of work on the present perfect.

Acknowledgments

Sue Lake originated this activity.

Contributor

Patricia Brenner, Teacher Educator and ESL Instructor at the University of Washington, is presently a Fulbright scholar at Bilkent University in Ankara, Turkey.

Be Honest

Levels
Low intermediate

Aims
Practice the simple past and present perfect tenses through questions about students' real-life experiences

Class Time
15 minutes

Preparation Time
Almost none

Students contrast the present perfect and past tenses by forming questions with *Have you ever?* and then probing for details of *when, where,* and *why,* using the past tense.

Procedure

1. Use the questions below to develop other questions:

   Have you ever . . .
   put your hand in someone else's pocket?
   worn someone else's trousers?
   run after someone?
   lied to someone?
   bought a ring?
   broken anything?
   spoken to a policewoman?
   drunk too much?

2. Ask the students to think about the question. Then ask someone if they have ever done whatever it is. Do not accept no for an answer unless it is really true. Then follow up with further questions as to *when, how, why, with whom,* and so on.

Caveats and Options

1. The students can produce their own questions and complete the activity in pairs.
2. Be careful not to include questions that are too personal or culturally sensitive.

Contributors

Anthony Bruton has trained teachers in Brazil, Spain and Singapore and is Associate Lecturer in methodology at the University of Seville, Spain. Angeles Broca teaches English in a vocational secondary school in the state system near Seville, Spain.

Super Bingo

Levels
Beginning–low
intermediate

Aims
Practice asking *Have
you ever* . . . ? questions
while developing peer
relationships

Class Time
15–30 minutes

Preparation Time
5 minutes

Resources
Super Bingo Sheet (see
Appendix)

This activity improves the mastery of questions with the present perfect in a bingo game format.

Procedure

1. Start by introducing yourself naturally, but be sure to mention the following: a food you like to eat, a music form you like to listen to, a foreign country or city you have visited, a domestic sight you have visited, and a sport you like to play. You may want to list these topics on the board as you mention them.
2. Draw a bingo sheet on the board with the normal numbers and letters, and demonstrate how the game is played. If bingo is alien to the cultures of most of your students, you can demonstrate it quickly.
3. Then erase the letters and explain that they will be replaced by the topics from your introduction and the numbers will be replaced by the answers.
4. Present the question and answer patterns necessary for filling out the sheet so students can successfully complete the activity. The questions are listed below the Super Bingo Sheet for reference.
5. Put the students in pairs to fill out the squares on the Super Bingo Sheet. They do this by asking each other questions using the models provided. There are five answers per topic. The answers must be the same for each partner. In other words, the pairs must find five types of food that both partners have eaten.
6. Finally, have the students move all of the furniture out of the way and roam about the room individually asking other students questions that lead to answers that match their own. They do this until someone gets Bingo by matching five answers in a line—vertically, horizontally, or diagonally. The only rule is that students can only ask another student one question at a time and must then move on to another student.

Caveats and Options

1. Eliminate the pair work of Step 5. This is really just a bit of extra pair work designed to raise the student comfort level.
2. You can choose a set of topics of your own if you think they will help the students successfully accomplish the task.
3. You can change the question form to practice a different grammatical form.
4. Because the students can be told that the main point of this activity is to get to know one another, and you merely circulate around the room giving encouragement and not correcting errors, they should have little fear of expressing themselves.
5. Many ESL classes comprise students with a variety of characterizing and nationalities. We do our students, and ourselves as teachers, a great service by breaking the ice early so all of the students can talk to classmates with whom they have something in common.

Acknowledgments

This activity was adapted from an ice breaker lesson. The author wishes to thank David Freitas for his suggestions, ideas and demonstrations while they worked together in Tokyo.

Appendix: Super Bingo Sheet

Bingo Sheet

Foreign City	Food Eaten	Music Type	Domestic Site Visited	Sport Played
		Free		

Questions
Have you ever been to *(foreign country or city)*?
Have you ever eaten *(type of food)*?
Have you ever visited *(domestic site)*?
Have you ever listened to *(music type)*?
Have you ever played *(sport)*?

Contributor

Patrick F. Colabucci is Supervisor in the English Education Department of TAC Co., Ltd., Tokyo, Japan, and a student in the Temple University of Japan MA in TESL course.

◆ Past Perfect Action Sequences

Levels
High intermediate

Aims
Clarify the use of the past perfect tense in extended discourse
Contrast the past perfect tense with the simple past and past progressive forms

Class Time
1 hour

Preparation Time
10 minutes

Resources
VCR and a copy of the James Bond movie, *The Man With the Golden Gun*

This activity practices the past perfect tense in extended discourse and clarifies tense contrasts by using popular films.

Procedure

1. Make one copy of the video summary for each pair of students (see Appendix).
2. Introduce the James Bond video by showing a few minutes of the movie with the sound turned off. Have students guess who the characters are, where the movie is taking place, and what is happening. Most students are familiar with the Bond movies, so this is usually easy for them.
3. Play the segment from the time Bond wakes up in the martial arts school through his escape across the bridge. Then have the students summarize the basic story line. Help them with any new vocabulary, but do not highlight any incorrect tense usage at this point.
4. Hand out copies of the summary, and have pairs of students fill in the blanks using any appropriate verb tense.
5. Check the students' choices by replaying the video segment, if necessary, to show the time relationships between events. For example, students will see that Bond was hit on the head before he fell asleep. Therefore, the past perfect tense form (*had hit*) would be appropriate. Likewise, Bond was in the middle of drinking his tea when the karate performance began, hence the need for the past progressive tense (as in *he was drinking*).
6. For a practice activity, have students watch another 5-minute segment of the movie, and in pairs, write their own summaries using appropriate tenses.

74

Caveats and Options

1. Students should be familiar with the simple past and past progressive tenses before they try this activity.
2. This activity works well with other movies, particularly those that are action-packed and have clearly defined sequences of events. *Jurassic Park* would also be an excellent source for this action sequence activity. Other suggestions might be the *Raiders of the Lost Ark* series, *Star Wars*, *Star Trek*, and other Bond movies.
3. Video segments can also be used to highlight other grammar points such as conditionals (*If Bond hadn't jumped out of the window, he wouldn't have escaped*) and modals (*Schula shouldn't have turned his back on Bond*).

Appendix: The Man With the Golden Gun Handout

The Man With the Golden Gun
Video Segment Summary
(Count No. 1145-1500)

At the beginning of this segment, James Bond (wake up) _____ in a martial arts school. He (realizes) _____ that he (sleep) _____ for some time, probably because someone (hit) _____ him over the head the night before.

Anyway, while Bond (relax) _____ and (drink) _____ some tea, the karate experts (begin) _____ to perform. Soon after, one of the students (invite) _____ Bond to join him, and seeing that it would be difficult to refuse, Bond (agree) _____.

They (step) _____ onto the mat together and (bow) _____ to one another, but just as the student (straighten up) _____, Bond (knock) _____ him out.

Consequently, Bond (have to) _____ face Schula, the best fighter in the school, and a man who (never/defeat) _____ before. Dealing with Schula was a lot more difficult, but eventually Bond (manage) _____ to throw Schula to the ground, and by the time Schula (turn) _____ around, Bond (jump) _____out of the window.

Luckily, Bond's friend Lee and his two nieces were there to help him. They (pick) _____ Bond up, and (escape) _____ when several students (appear) _____ and (block) _____ their path. However, there was no need to worry. Lee's nieces were karate experts, and by the time Bond (realize) _____ what was happening, the girls (knock out) _____ all their pursuers.

Contributor

Jane Dresser is Senior Instructor in ESL at Portland State University, Oregon, in the United States.

Past Perfect Game

Levels
Intermediate

Aims
Use the past perfect
tense appropriately

Class Time
50 minutes

Preparation Time
None

Resources
None

Students ask and answer questions as part of a game to practice using the past perfect tense.

Procedure

1. Ask a student to volunteer some information about his or her life and write a sample timeline on the board using the past tense, including a variety of events, for example: *enrolled in school, left Vietnam, joined the volleyball team.*
2. Erase sample timeline. Ask several other student volunteers to write similar timelines about their own lives on the board. The rest of the class follows what they write and asks questions about anything that is not clear to them.
3. Divide the class into two teams. One half of each team is responsible for asking questions and the other half for answering questions. Then number questioners and answerers.
4. Advise students that they must use one of the timelines to ask a question using the past perfect tense, for example, *Where had Lee studied English before he came to this school? How long had Trinh lived in the refugee camp before she came to this country?* In order to score a point, they must get both the grammar and the information according to the timeline correct. The same rule applies to those answering the questions. (Alternatively, one could award two points, one for the grammar and one for the timeline information.) No question may be asked more than once.
5. Toss a coin to decide which team starts. The team that wins the toss is named Team A and the other team, Team B (or other names of your choice). Questioner 1 from Team A starts the game by asking Answerer 1 of Team B a question. Award points as indicated above and listed on the board. Then Questioner 1 from Team B asks Answerer

1 of Team A a question, and so on until every student has had an opportunity to ask or answer a question. If the class does not divide evenly, the extra person can be the scorekeeper.

6. Tally the score and acknowledge the winning team.

Caveats and Options

1. If you would like to have some control over the timelines, assign all the students to write them for homework beforehand and then select those to be put on the board.

2. The game may be used to practice other tenses. Because the past tense is frequently an acceptable alternative to the past perfect, it is your prerogative to decide which verb forms to accept, that is, to establish the rules of the game.

Contributor

Margaret Grant teaches in the ESL program at San Francisco State University, California, in the United States.

What Had Happened Before?

Levels
High intermediate

Aims
Contextualize the past
perfect through
historical events

Class Time
Varies

Preparation Time
20 minutes

Resources
An account of
Magellan's
circumnavigation of the
world or another
famous explorer's/
traveller's life story
Suitable wall map
Index cards

Referring to achievements in a famous person's life, students contrast the past perfect with the simple past.

Procedure

1. Choose important dates from the life story you selected.
2. Prepare cards with the date and a brief reference to the event.
3. In class, put the map of the world on the board and as you give an account of the trip attach the relevant card near the place of occurrence on the map.
4. When you finish your account, offer sample statements. For example: *By the time Magellan reached the Philippines, he had been at sea . . .*
5. After several examples, ask students to form similar statements based on the cards you have attached to the map.

Caveats and Options

1. You may wish to assign a short written account of the same trip for homework.
2. A variation on this activity or a subsequent assignment may be to ask each student to interview an older acquaintance or family member about their life history and then present it to the class in a similar manner, using instead of the wall map a "life road," which each student constructs based on the interviewee's life story.

Contributor

Lily Vered is currently in charge of teacher education and materials development of a large scale project at the Open University of Israel.

◆ Conditionals
The Beautiful Princess

Levels
Intermediate

Aims
Preview and reinforce
the future conditional
by having students
create a story

Class Time
10–15 minutes

Preparation Time
None

Resources
Chalkboard or overhead
projector (OHP)

Using the mnemonic story idea (see "The Party," p. 47], students work on *if*-clauses expressing future conditionals by developing a story in which they figure as characters.

Procedure

1. Set the scene:

   Do you know the story about the beautiful princess? There once was a princess who was so beautiful that princes came from all over the world because they wanted to marry her. The princess always asked them the same question: "What will you give me if I marry you?"

   The first prince was the handsome prince from (Name the nationality of one of your students and indicate him). The princess (Indicate a female student) asked him: "What will you give me if I marry you?" (She asks the question—other students help her as necessary). And he said, "I will give you a gold ring if you marry me. But I won't if you don't." (Elicit the negative with gestures and perhaps help from other students.)

   The next prince . . . (Indicate student). The princess (Indicate another female) asked him, "What will you give me if I marry you?" and he said, "I will give you a white horse if you marry me. But I won't if you don't."

2. Ask other students: "What did she ask him? What did he say in reply"?
3. The story continues for as long as you wish. You may of course use false nationalities or have students supply nationalities.
4. At the end of the story, ask: "What time are we talking about? (future) What word did we use in each example? (*if*) Who will the princess marry? (Here the students tend to be too involved in the content to

79

be focused on the meaning of *if*.) We don't know. When do we use *if*? In the future to indicate that we don't know."

7. On board or overhead projector: Ask students to generate the basic structures:

FUTURE	IF	PRESENT
What will you give me	IF	I marry you?
I will give you a gold ring	IF	you marry me.
But I won't	IF	you don't.

Caveats and Options

1. The story format can be used to introduce or to review the future conditional.
2. This activity offers an opportunity to practice the pronunciation of *won't*.
3. The students tell the story, not the teacher.
4. If a student misuses the structure at a later date, the teacher can say: "Remember the princess."

Acknowledgments

Sue Lake deserves joint credit for this idea.

Contributor

Patricia Brenner, Teacher Educator and ESL Instructor at the University of Washington, is presently a Fulbright scholar at Bilkent University in Ankara, Turkey.

Be Another

Levels
Low intermediate

Aims
Practice the hypothetical conditional

Class Time
10 minutes

Preparation Time
Almost none

Resources
None

Students practice the conditional with questions about being someone else.

Procedure

The students, in pairs, make up conditional questions beginning *what/who*, using the prompts below. When their partner replies, they ask a *why* question.

For example

> What nationality would you be, if you could be any?
> Why?
> Prompts: any nationality
>   any city
>   any name
>   any girlfriend/boyfriend
>   any ability
>   either gender
>   any number of brother and sisters

Caveats and Options

1. The learners could guess their partners' choice, and then ask the why question. For example, *Would you be Jamaican?*
2. To make the process quicker, the partner can say if the guess is very close, close, or not close.

Contributor

Anthony Bruton has trained teachers in Brazil, Spain, and Singapore and is Associate Lecturer in methodology at the University of Seville, Spain.

Guess Who, What, Where

Levels
Low intermediate

Aims
Practice using
hypothetical
conditionals through a
guessing game

Class Time
10 minutes upwards

Preparation Time
Almost none

Resources
None

Contributor

Students practice the conditional by asking yes/no questions to guess what their partner is thinking of.

Procedure

One student in a pair thinks of a country, a city, a person, or a type of food, and the other tries to guess it, using yes/no questions beginning with *if*.

> If I ate it, would I need a fork?
> If I ate it, would I burn my tongue?
> If I wanted to, could I use my hands?

Caveats and Options

Students can never use nationalities in the questions.

Anthony Bruton has trained teachers in Brazil, Spain, and Singapore and is Associate Lecturer in methodology at the University of Seville, Spain.

Problem-Solving Task for Conditionals

Levels
Intermediate

Aims
Practice the conditional
through communicative
task performance and
solve a grammar
problem inductively

Class Time
50–65 minutes

Preparation Time
1–2 hours

Resources
A variety of grammar
textbooks and teacher
references (see
References and Further
Reading)

This activity employs an information gap task to raise students' consciousness of how to use present and future conditional forms with *if*.

Procedure

1. The classroom should be organized for pair work. In those rooms where the furniture is arranged in rows and cannot be moved, the students should work with those sitting behind them.
2. Students should take the pretest first and score their answers. The pretest is followed by performance of the task.
3. After they've finshed the task, different students should read their answers to the task questions and present their rules for use of the grammar structure. Give feedback on the correctness of the sentences and the grammar rules. You may wish to give a more detailed explanation of the structure and additional examples.
4. After discussion of the task, the students should take the posttest and score their answers.

Caveats and Options

1. The task may be performed in small groups (thus requiring some rewriting of the task sheet) or may be done as a teacher-fronted activity.
2. You may want to grade the pre-/posttest or ask students to rewrite the incorrect sentences.
3. This activity can be done as part of a communicative lesson, to be followed by meaning-focused activities containing the target structure, or can be used in a more traditional classroom setting to combine communicative language use with formal grammar study.

References and Further Reading

Celce-Murcia, M., & Larsen-Freeman, D. (1983). *The grammar book.* Cambridge, MA: Newbury House.

Fotos, S., Homan, R., & Poel, C. (1994). *Grammar in mind: Communicative English for fluency and accuracy.* Tokyo: Logos.

Nunan, D. (1989). *Designing tasks for the communicative classroom.* Cambridge: Cambridge University Press.

Appendix A: *If*-Conditional Pre-/Posttest

A. Grammaticality Judgment Section

Students should indicate which sentences are correct and which are incorrect. They may also be asked to rewrite any incorrect sentences.

1. _____ Would I save money if I took the bus instead of the train?
2. _____ I will call you right away if I find your keys.
3. _____ If Tom runs in the next race, he will probably win.
4. _____ If Jan would be taller, could she play basketball?
5. _____ If I would hurry, I will be on time.
6. _____ If you were rich, you will travel all over the world.
7. _____ We would go to the North Pole if we had the chance?
8. _____ I would be happy if I won first prize in the Speech Contest.
9. _____ Maria would arrive at noon if she takes the 10:45 bus.
10. _____ If it will rain tomorrow, our picnic will be cancelled.

B. Sentence Production Section

Students should make a sentence using the words given below. (For reference, the correct sentences are given in parentheses; the *if* clause can be used at the beginning or end of the sentence.)

1. he   car   if   refuse   my   asked   to   borrow   I   would
   (If he asked to borrow my car, I would refuse.)

2. taxi they is a take will late the train if
(If the train is late, they will take a taxi.)

_____

3. would we rich everywhere if travel were we
(If we were rich, we would travel everywhere.)

_____

4. I be dinosaur if I frightened saw a would
(If I saw a dinosaur, I would be frightened.)

_____

5. yourself movie you will exciting enjoy see if happy you
(If you see that exciting movie, you will enjoy yourself.)

_____

Appendix B: *If*-Conditional Grammar Task Sheet

Task Sheet: Student A

In this task, you will make sentences using *if*. Work in pairs.

Directions: Take turns asking each other the questions below. Write your partner's answers on the lines and check that they are correct. All answers should use "if". When you have finished, write the rules for the correct word order and correct verb use for each type of *if*-conditional sentence.

1. Talk about a possible event in the present or future, something that could happen. For example:

Question: What will happen if I don't drive carefully?
Answer: If you don't drive carefully, you will probably have an accident.

Question 1: What will you do if you have an English test in two days?
Answer: _____

Question 2: Where will you go if you take a trip during the summer vacation?
Answer: _____

Rule for making correct sentences about events that will probably happen:
(Use these words: *subject, present tense verb phrase, will*)

_____

2. Talk about an imaginary event in the present or future, something that is not very possible. For example:

Question: What would you do if you had a million dollars?
Answer: If I had a million dollars, I would save it all.

Question 1: If you could live anywhere in the world, where would you live?
Answer: _____

Question 2: What would you do if I asked you for all your money?
Answer: _____

Rule for making correct sentences about imaginary events that would not be likely to happen. (Use these words: *subject, past tense verb phrase, would*)

_____

Appendix C: *If*-Conditional Grammar Task Sheet

Task Sheet: Student B

In this task you will make sentences using *if*. Work in pairs.
Directions: Take turns asking each other the questions below. Write your partner's answers on the lines and check that they are correct. All answers should use *if*. When you have finished, write the rules for correct word order and correct verb use for each type of *if*-conditional sentence.

1. Talk about a possible event in the present or future, something that could happen. For example:

Question: What will happen if I don't drive carefully?
Answer: If you don't drive carefully, you will probably have an accident.

Question 1: Where will you eat if you have dinner at a restaurant tonight?
Answer: _____

Question 2: What will happen if you don't pay your telephone bill?
Answer: _____

Rule for making correct sentences about events that will probably happen:
(Use these words: *subject, present tense verb phrase, will*)

_____

2. Talk about an imaginary event in the present or future, something that is not very possible. For example:

Question: What would you do if you had a million dollars?
Answer: If I had a million dollars, I would save it all.

Question 1: Where would you go if you could visit another planet?
Answer: _____

Question 2: What would happen if you were asked to be a movie star?
Answer: _____

Rule for making correct sentences about imaginary events that are not very possible.
(Use these words: *subject, past tense verb phrase, would*)

_____

Contributor

Sandra S. Fotos is Associate Professor at Senshu University, Tokyo, Japan.

If I Had a Hammer

Levels
Intermediate +

Aims
Practice counterfactual
conditionals in a
realistic context

Class Time
20–50 minutes

Preparation Time
None

Resources
Any handy objects
provided by the
classroom setting, you,
or the students
Recording of song "If I
Had a Hammer" and a
machine to play it on
(optional)

Students make hypothetical statements about what they would, could, or might do with certain objects as a way to practice the counterfactual conditional.

Procedure

1. (optional) Play "If I Had a Hammer."
2. Put sample sentences on the board for counterfactual conditionals with *have* in the *if*-clause:

   If I *had* a hammer, *I'd hammer* in the morning.
   If I *had* a bell, *I'd ring* it in the morning.

3. Pick out an object that a student has but that you don't have and model sentences on the board such as:

   If I *had* that briefcase, *I'd fill* it up with your assignments and mark them at home.
   If *I had* a green sweater, *I'd buy* a nice green skirt to go with it.

4. Display items on a table in front of the class or have students display items on their desks.
5. Call on a student to select an object and to make a statement about the object in the counterfactual pattern. Assist the student if needed.
6. Let that student call on the next student and continue until each one has at least one chance to make a sentence.
7. (optional) Play "If I Had a Hammer" again and let students sing along.

Caveats and Options

1. The activity can be elaborated or built on in a subsequent class period by allowing variations on the pattern, such as verbs other than *have*

and subjects other than *I* in the *if*-clause, and structure other than *I'd* in the main clause, for example,

If you gave me that ring, then we would be engaged.
If Carlos refused to lend me $10, I could not be friends with him any more.

2. The oral activity can be followed up by a written activity, either writing individual sentences or a paragraph beginning, *If I had a million dollars* . . . .

Contributor

Martha C. Pennington is University Reader (Research Coordinator) in English at the City Polytechnic of Hong Kong.

◆ Sequence of Tenses
Verb Sequencing With a Penguin

Levels
Beginning–intermediate

Aims
Work on progressive
tenses in a motivating
visual, kinetic, and
concrete context

Class Time
10–20 minutes

Preparation Time
10–15 minutes

Resource
Wind-up plastic
penguin

A wind-up penguin elicits commands, questions, and answers that describe actions.

Procedure

1. Wind up the penguin to walk around or make it appear to walk on top of a desk or table (the ice). Use a small box or dish for the nest.
2. First demonstrate what the penguin is doing, with running narration.
3. Then ask the students questions to elicit sentences.
4. Students often will then say sentences, so you can have the penguin do what they are saying (TPR = Total Penguin Response).

Caveats and Options

This exercise might be thought of as Total Physical Response Revisited; the language examples are given so that students can figure out the rules inductively and then apply them to give orders or narration.

Appendix: Sample Classroom Dialogue

The penguin is walking. She was walking, but now she has stopped. What is she looking for? Her nest? Yes, she is looking for her nest. She is still looking for her nest. She has been walking for a long time, and she is getting tired. Aha! what has she found? Yes, she has found her nest!

Where is she going now? Right, she is going towards the sea [off the desk]. She is going near the edge of the cliff. [make her dive off the edge gracefully] She is . . . . (Students: "Jump!" "Dive"!) yes, she is diving into the water. Oh no! There's a leopard seal in the water! The leopard seal is chasing her! The penguin wants to escape! She is swimming back toward the ice. She is swimming faster and faster. She has reached the ice! She is safe!

Contributor

Lise Winer is Associate Professor in the Department of Linguistics, Southern Illinois University, Carbondale, in the United States.

◆ General Tenses Grammar Match Up

Levels
Intermediate +

Aims
Recognize specific grammar points and their usage in a communicative and gamelike atmosphere

Class Time
10–20 minutes

Preparation Time
20 minutes

Resources
One blank card (or piece of paper)/student

This card-matching activity practices recognition of proper tense forms.

Procedure

1. Prepare two sets of cards. The first set will have a particular tense (e.g., past, present perfect) written on it. The second will have sentences in which various tense forms are used.
2. Give each student a card. If there are more cards than students, make sure that you give each companion card to a different student.
3. Have students move about the room attempting to find their partners. Remind the students not just to read the cards, but to communicate with the other students to solve the activity.
4. After all of the students have found their partners, the students with the tense card should tell the class which tense they have, and the students with the sentence card should respond by reading the sentence with the proper tense form of the verb.
5. If time remains, reshuffle the cards and let the students do the activity again for reinforcement.
6. When the activity has been completed, the students can pin their cards next to each other on a bulletin board. This allows the students to refer to the cards during breaks and before or after class for the next few days.

Caveats and Options

1. Use other types of grammar points. For example, the teaching of word classes would lend itself well to this type of activity. Half the cards would have a specific word class, and the other half would have words or phrases illustrating those classes.

2. After the students have successfully performed this type of matching activity, give them more responsibility. The next time the activity is used, have the students prepare the cards and run the activity themselves. The time after that, let them choose the particular grammar point to learn.
3. Grammar Match Ups work well as warm-up activities. Students should already be familiar with the different tense forms prior to using this activity.

Contributor

Thomas Nixon teaches in the American English Institute at California State University, Fresno, and is a candidate for the Master of Arts in Linguistics (ESL Option) at that university.

Tense and Time Mapping

Levels
Intermediate +

Aims
Review the use of
tenses and see
relationship between
tense and time

Class Time
Varies

Preparation Time
10–15 minutes

Resources
Any article (from the
newspaper, magazines,
students' discipline of
studies) that
incorporates various
tenses

Tense-time relationships are graphed in relation to real texts.

Procedure

1. Choose a suitable passage of interest to students.
2. Prepare a timeline representing events as covered in the text. Use a standard grammar reference book for timeline formats. For lengthy texts, you may underline the verbs to be mapped.
3. Distribute reading passage to students and check for comprehension.
4. Students map the verbs in relation to the time expressed over the set time frame.
5. Students may discuss their map with their classmates (or discussion may be teacher fronted on an overhead projector).
6. Highlight the range in the use of tenses and their aspects to convey information in relation to time.

Caveats and Options

1. Choose a restricted time frame in the text (e.g., one day in a text that spans 5 days) and highlight all the different tenses used to describe the activities that happened and their relation in time.
2. This activity is very helpful when done with texts that cover a range of time spans, for example, 2 hours versus 2 weeks.

Contributor

Jasbir Pannu is Lecturer in the Division of Humanities and Social Sciences, College of Higher Vocational Studies, City Polytechnic of Hong Kong.

Part IV: Modal Verbs

Modal Exchanges

Levels
High intermediate +

Aims
Practice using modal verbs appropriately and spontaneously

Class Time
30 minutes

Preparation Time
Varies

Resources
1 reference sheet for each referee (see Appendices)
1 game sheet for each player (more if they want to play several times with different people)
1 set of cards for each pair of players

This activity gives high intermediate and advanced students of English a context in which to practice using modal verbs.

Procedure

1. Organize students in groups of three: two players and one referee.
2. Tell students the game's objective: to reach the center line before the opponent.
3. Shuffle cards and place them upside down on the table.
4. The first player picks a card and using the modal verb on the card starts a conversation on any one of the eight topics marked on the game sheet. (The modal verb can be used in any form—e.g., question, negative, past). The topic chosen is not stated.
5. If the referee accepts what is said as correct, both players shade in one square in the relevant topic column on the relevant half of the game sheet, that is, *Me* or *My Opponent*.
6. The second player then picks a card and, using the modal verb on the card, responds to the first player and then states the topic. If the referee accepts what is said as grammatically correct, both players shade in one square in the relevant column on the relevant half of the game sheet. If the second player has also chosen the correct topic, another square is shaded. One exchange has then been completed.
7. The next exchange is then started by the second player, who picks a card and starts a conversation on any topic, and the exchange continues.
8. The winner of the game is the one who succeeds in shading all the squares for any one of the topics, as far as the center line on the *Me* side.

Caveats and Options

1. A game requires some suspension of disbelief, and thus a language game may not produce genuine communication. However, a game scenario can enable the language teacher to focus on particular aspects of language production.
2. The activity is intended to be used after a presentation session and to be followed up by communicative activities.
3. The game scenario allows the students to use a variety of modal verbs, quickly and under pressure, while still having fun.

Appendix A: Modal Exchanges (Reference Sheet)

WILL	*Is that the doorbell? It will be my brother ....* *If litmus paper is dipped in acid, it will* *turn red* *You will become a millionaire*	} PREDICTION
	I will leave on Friday.	INTENTION
	I will do it for you.	WILLINGNESS
	Will you do that for me?	REQUEST
MUST	*Our guests must be home by now*	CERTAINTY
	You must be back by 2 o'clock.	speaker's authority
	I must phone my parents	} OBLIGATION speaker's authority over himself
CAN	*Can I come in?*	PERMISSION
	Can you help me?	REQUEST
	Your work can be improved	theoretical
	Overwork can be dangerous	} POSSIBILITY sometimes
	He can speak English fluently	
	Can you drive a car?	} ABILITY
SHOULD	*You should see a doctor.*	ADVICE
	All students should be punctual	OBLIGATION
	He should be home by now	PROBABILITY
COULD	*Could I see you for a few minutes*	PERMISSION
	They could have seen your purse	theoretical
	In those days a man could be hung *for stealing a sheep*	} POSSIBILITY sometimes
	He could play the piano when he was five ...	ABILITY (past)
ABLE TO	*He's able to do simultaneous translation ......*	
	Will you be able to meet us at 8?	} ABILITY
MAY	*May I come in?*	PERMISSION
	I may have dropped it	
	The social services may be improved	} POSSIBILITY
MIGHT	*Might I ask your opinion?*	PERMISSION
	They might have seen your purse	POSSIBILITY
HAVE TO	*You have to be joking!*	CERTAINTY
	You have to be back by 2 o'clock	
	I have to phone my parents	
	The had to work a 50-hour week	} OBLIGATION (3rd party authority)
OUGHT TO	*I ought to phone my parents*	OBLIGATION
	Our guests ought to be home by now	
	This game ought to be simple to play!	} PROBABILITY

Appendix B: Sample Game Sheet

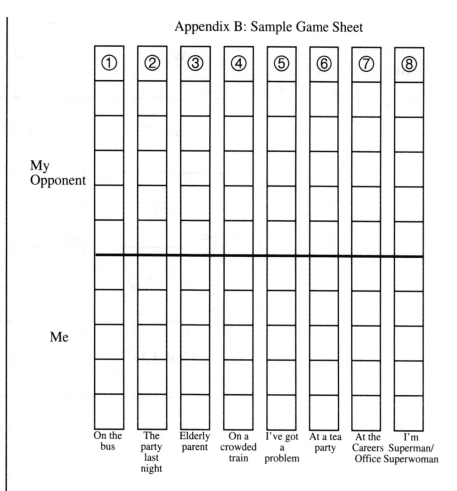

Appendix B: Sample Game Sheet

**Appendix C:
Sample Cards**

WILL	MAY
MUST	MIGHT
CAN	HAVE TO
SHOULD	ABLE TO
COULD	OUGHT TO

Contributor

Wendy E. Ball is EFL Tutor at the Institute for Applied Language Studies, University of Edinburgh in the United Kingdom.

All You Have to Do Is Ask

Levels
Beginning

Aims
Practice making
common requests with
May I . . . ?; Can I . . . ?
Use request grammar
without overt emphasis
on form

Class Time
20–25 minutes

Preparation Time
10 minutes

Resources
List of verbs commonly
used in classroom
requests

Procedure

1. Write the verb list on the board and go over the list with the class. Because the main focus is on grammar, it is important not to get bogged down in vocabulary. Use words that the students know or can handle easily (e.g., *borrow, turn on, turn off, open, close, erase, write , ask, sit, leave, use, put on, take off, read*).
2. Students take turns making requests of each other, using the words on the board. Student A begins by saying the name of another student and making a request of that student. However, Student A must give some kind of reason for the request. In addition, Student B must give a linguistically (and physically) correct response.

A: Carol, I forgot my dictionary. May I borrow your dictionary?
B: Sure. (She hands him the dictionary.) Here you are.
A: Mike, it's hot in here. May I open the window?
B: (He nods his head.) Sure. Go ahead.

Caveats and Options

1. This activity can be carried out without requiring students to perform the physical response. The suitability of having students perform the physical action depends on your familiarity with what is appropriate as well as the students' level of inhibition. I have found that students (especially Japanese students) have a good time trying to mimic what English speakers do when they give certain responses.
2. Coming up with reasons for a request is not easy to do on the spot, so you might want to have students write out several reasons plus requests as a homework assignment.

3. One of the main benefits of this activity is that it equips students with language that they can and will use in the classroom as they deal with their classmates throughout the rest of the term. Students usually get so caught up in verbalizing their reasons that they pay little attention to the target pattern of may/can and thus make very few mistakes with this pattern.

Contributor

Nadine Battaglia is Instructor of English and French at the Language Academy, Maebashi, Japan.

You Make the Rules

Levels
Intermediate +

Aims
Practice making positive
and negative statements
of obligation using
*must, have to, is
required to, should, will,
if-*clauses, and
imperatives

Class Time
20–30 minutes

Preparation Time
10 minutes

Students make up sets of rules to cover different types of situations as a way to practice modals of obligation and related structures.

Procedure

1. Identify appropriate situations where students could make up their own rules about how to behave, for example, do's and dont's for behaving in the classroom, the school library, the playground, the family home.
2. Choose a situation that would be suitable for the age and interests of your learners, preferably one that is fun and not too serious.
3. Explain to the students that they must generate a set of rules for that situation. To clarify the task, give examples of the kind of structures they should use. For example, In the family home:

   Rule 1. The last person to finish dinner has to wash up all the dishes.
   Rule 2. If anyone forgets to make her bed, she has to make everyone else's bed the next day.

4. Set a time limit. Students work on their rules. One student is the group scribe and writes down the rules as they are generated by the group. Move around and give feedback as needed.
5. The whole class reassembles and the group scribes reads out their rules.
6. Students from other groups are invited to give their opinions of the rules after they have been read out by each group. Do they accept the suggested rules? Have a short class discussion as appropriate.
7. After all the rules have been read out and discussed, the class votes on which group has produced the most interesting set of rules.

Contributor

Dino Mahoney is University Lecturer at the City Polytechnic of Hong Kong.

Discussing Disasters

Levels
Intermediate +

Aims
Practice past modals
*should have, could
have, must have, might
have,* and *would have*
in a realistic context

Class Time
50 minutes

Preparation Time
30 minutes

Resources
Magazine accounts of
disasters (e.g., from
Newsweek, Time, Life)

Students practice past modals by simulating a debate between two insurance companies as to which party was at fault in a disaster.

Procedure

1. Make copies of the magazine article for every student.
2. Present the disaster to the class in some engaging manner. (For example, for the crash of two 747s in Tenerife on the Canary Islands in 1977, I taped a model runway on the classroom floor and two students manipulated two cardboard planes as two others read aloud an adaptation of the radio messages between the planes and the tower described in the news article.)
3. Divide the class into groups, each representing the insurance company for one of the parties concerned. In the case of the Canary Islands disaster, one group represented Pan Am, one represented KLM, and one represented the Tenerife Airport.
4. After designating a group leader and a group speaker, each group discusses why it is not at fault and how it can avoid higher insurance premiums for the party it represents.
5. Each group's speaker presents its arguments to the whole class.
6. Debate among the parties then occurs, with everyone in each group participating at will.
7. The class as a whole votes on which group presented the best argument.
8. Ask the students to write up their views of the disaster as a follow-up assignment.

Caveats and Options

1. Show a videotape or magazine pictures of the disaster so that there is as much information available as possible.
2. In the final discussion, the students will make spontaneous use of the past modals or some approximation to them because what they have to do is report on an undesirable matter that is already past. At this point, decide if and when it would be beneficial to engage the class in some grammatical consciousness raising about the way that actions that should have been taken (but were not) are reported in English. If you notice that the students are having trouble with this area of grammar while preparing their arguments, it might be a good idea to provide the whole class with some guidelines in grammatical usage concerning past modals before the final presentation is given.

Contributor

Peter Master is Associate Professor in the Department of Linguistics, California State University, Fresno, in the United States.

Abilities and Possibilities

Levels
High intermediate +

Aims
Practice expressing
necessity, ability,
possibility, probability,
and obligation
Encourage sensitivity
about disabilities,
making students aware
of the many activities
the disabled can engage
in successfully

Class Time
10–30 minutes

Preparation Time
15 minutes

Resources
Catalogues, brochures,
and magazines that
might carry photographs
of people with
disabilities fuctioning in
everyday situations (see
References and Further
Reading)

Students practice modal verbs and all types of question and response forms based on pictures of people with disabilities participating in leisure and work-related activities.

Procedure

1. Choose a picture of a disabled person, engaged in an activity, if possible.
2. Enlarge the picture, if necessary, so that the whole class can see it.
3. As students look at the picture, make comments and ask questions about the situation presented, using modals.
4. Follow up initial questions with *how? why?* and other information questions which require exposition and/or argumentation.
5. With more advanced students, ask the students to speculate on the disabled person's past and future.
6. As the class discusses the safety and courtesy aspects of each situation, they should decide what is most appropriate from the point of view of the disabled person and the others involved.
7. The class might also discuss how this situation would be handled in their native countries.

Appendix: Sample Situations and Questions

1. A picture of a basketball player in wheelchair: Can he swim? Live alone? Ride a bus? Shop in a supermarket? // (past time) As a child, go to his neighborhood school? Go to school social events? Enroll in physical education classes? Go to summer camp? Take part in his graduation?// (future) Work as a teacher? As a salesman? As an engineer? As a doctor? Get married? Be an effective father? Travel overseas (to your country)?

106

2. A picture of a blind student on campus: Should she live in a dormitory? Get a dog? Go on dates? Walk briskly? Go out when it is snowy or icy? Go to the beach and swim in the ocean? // (past time) Be sent to a regular school? Play with sighted or with other blind children? Ride a bicycle? // (future time) After she finishes school, get married? Have children? Ride on an airplane alone? Get a job in an office? In a hotel?

Other Possible Options

Present pictures of the following people and elicit discussion using the modals indicated:

1. Outdoor worker with disability: must (necessity)
2. Woman with working dog and skis: must (probability)
3. Person using wheelchair at intersection: may (permission)
4. Group with disabilities at tourist attraction: may (possibility)
5. Paraplegic teacher talking with student
6. Wheelchair-using businessman taking the bus
7. Injured person rescued from fire
8. Accident (resulting in injury) hospital patient

Caveats and Options

1. These same procedures can be carried out in groups. Also, reading and writing assignments could evolve from the oral activities.
2. Emphasis should be directed toward what the person can do, not what the person cannot do.
3. *The Americans with Disabilities Act Resource Catalog* emphasizes the problems the disabled have rather than their possible achievements. On the other hand, its material presents a greater variety of people with disabilities (amputees, the mentally retarded, the deaf) than the other materials.

References and Further Reading

The Americans with Disabilities Act Resource Catalog. National Easter Seal Society, 70 East Lake Street, Chicago, IL, 60601 (also available locally in some US cities), posters 17" x 24"; also video cassettes, audio cassettes, books, brochures.

CAREERS & the disABLED. Equal Opportunity Publications, Inc., 44 Broadway, Greenlawn, NY 11740 (published 3 times per year; contains pictures of disabled workers).

The Courtesy Rules of Blindness. National Federation of the Blind, 1800 Johnson St., Baltimore, MD 21230.

Wheelchair Etiquette. Schoit Medical Center, Waterloo, IA.

Acknowledgments

Thanks are due Alice Nagle, Coordinator of the People with Disabilities Program at the University of Pennsylvania, for her generous help in giving suggestions and in devoting a considerable amount of time in helping to assemble materials.

Contributor

Margaret Fenimore Petty is the Intensive Program Coordinator in the English Language Program at the University of Pennsylvania, in the United States.

What Could I Do?

Levels
Intermediate–high
intermediate

Aims
Elicit use of past modals
in realistic situations

Class Time
3–5 minutes/student

Preparation Time
20 minutes

Resources
Personal experience

Drawing on students' natural curiosity and their inclination to give advice, this activity reviews past tenses and past modals.

Procedure

1. Prepare enough cards, one per student, each describing very briefly an embarrassing or difficult situation.

   For example,

   - You took important guests to an expensive restaurant and when it was time to pay, you discovered you had no wallet.
   - You borrowed your friend's car promising to return it in the evening, but you had an accident.
   - Getting off the bus on the way to work, you suddenly ripped the back side of your slacks.

2. Seat students in a circle, sitting among them.
3. Hand each student a card, keeping one for yourself.
4. Allow students time to read their cards and prepare to tell the incident as if it had happened to them and they were telling their friends. Stories should end with *What could I do?* or *I had no idea what to do.*
5. After a student finishes his or her embarrassing/sad/funny story, the classmates acting as his or her friends, offer advice, for example:

   You could have offered to wash the dishes.
   You should have called home and asked the babysitter to send you the wallet by cab.

6. The student who told the story may respond as he or she sees fit, for example,

How could I? We had no babysitter.
What about my guests?

7. If no more advice is forthcoming, the next student to the left tells his or her story.
8. Tell your story first to provide an example.
9. As students interact, jot down errors for future remedial work and provide assistance with vocabulary when requested, but do not interfere with the activity.

Caveats and Options

1. If the group is large, create an inner circle, the members of which will recount the incidents on their cards, and an outer circle of friends giving advice.
2. To practice present tenses, provide present situations, with the final sentence of the account being *I don't know what to do*.
3. This activity is used to practice modals after students have mastered them as well as present and past tenses. The situations used should be familiar to the students so that they have enough vocabulary to deal with the activity imaginatively and with ease.

Contributor

Lily Vered is currently in charge of teacher education and materials development of a large scale project at the Open University of Israel.

Part V: Verb Complements

The Liar's Club

Levels
Intermediate +

Aims
Practice describing an object's function using *used for* + gerund, *used in* + gerund, *used* + infinitive and verb-to-noun transformation with *-er*

Class Time
Two 1-hour periods

Preparation Time
15 minutes

Resources
Functional items (e.g., can opener)

Students practice infinitives, gerunds, and nouns in *-er* by trying to guess the correct function of a particular object.

Procedure

Day 1

1. Show the class an object whose function is easily explained, such as a can opener, and elicit the language used to describe its function. Write this on the board. The most commonly used language to describe an object's function is:

   It's used to open cans. (infinitive)
   It's used for (in) opening cans. (gerund)
   It's a can open*er*. (verb to noun transformation with *-er*)

2. Show the class an object (or a piece of an object) whose function/use you think will be difficult for the students to guess. Objects that work well are things that are used when doing hobbies or one's job. Gizmos, gadgets, and pieces of appliances all work well to inspire the imagination. Give them four different explanations of the object's function (one should be true) using the different language structures previously presented.

3. In groups of three, students discuss which of the explanations is the true function/use of the object. Give each group 100 points to bet with. They can bet up to half of their points in each round, depending how certain they are as to which of your explanations is the true one. Play the game a few times if time permits.

4. Once the students understand the game and have the language needed for describing an object's use/function, ask them to bring a strange unidentifiable object (SUO) to the next class.

Day 2

1. Students now play Liar's Club in groups. Before they begin, review the language needed for describing an object's function. Then in groups students describe the function of the SUO they have brought to class and decide on three other believable explanations of the object's use.
2. The game is played as it was during the previous class, except that now a group gives its three explanations to the other groups, showing or passing each object to them. (The group giving the explanation should not feel obligated to pass around any object that they feel would make guessing the object's function too easy.)
3. After groups hear the explanations, they should discuss which explanation of the three is the true one and come to a group decision. For added interest they can place a bet, which can be up to one half of the points they currently have. Finally, the group with the SUO reveals which of the explanations of the object's use/function is the true one.
4. As the groups proceed in giving their three explanations, the teacher or a student keeps track of the points, and at the end of the game the group with the most points gets a round of applause (at least).

Caveats and Options

1. Because some students may have trouble finding appropriate objects, you can allow them to bring pictures of SUOs.
2. With classes of more than 16, you may want to pair two groups to work together for the duration of class.

Acknowledgments

This activity was adapted from a U.S. television show called "Liar's Club."

Contributor

Eric Bray is Academic Director of the Kyoto YMCA English School, in Japan.

Scrambled Gerunds and Infinitives in an Envelope

Levels
High intermediate +

Aims
Practice gerunds and
infinitives in a task-
based activity
Review grammatical
combinations of
gerunds and infinitives

Class Time
15–20 minutes

Preparation Time
15 minutes

Resources
Envelopes
Paper and pen
Scissors

In this alternative to traditional grammar book presentations, students work in groups to reconstruct sentences containing gerunds and infinitives.

Procedure

1. Write the following sentences on a sheet of paper. Leave ample space between the sentences. Cut the sentences into several pieces. Possible places to cut have been indicated with an asterisk (*).

   I don' t know how * you can * stand * getting up so early every day.
   No one enjoys * listening to classical music more * than Sam does.
   On the way home from the zoo, we persuaded * Jim * to stop * to eat.
   As soon as she * walked in the door, she could * smell something * burning.
   Our boss insists on * having all of us * clean our desks before * going home every day.
   If possible, I'd like * to avoid * driving in the noon traffic.
   Would you consider * letting John * use your car?

   The class will work in pairs or small groups. You will need one envelope with all 25 pieces per pair or small group.

2. Explain what a scrambled sentence is. If necessary, put an example on the board. (Write a sample sentence in three or four scrambled chunks. Have the students construct the correct sentence.)

3. Divide the class into pairs or groups. Have students clear one area of the table or desk so that everyone in the pair/group can help construct the sentences.

4. Give each pair/group an envelope. Have students empty the contents and count the number of sentence pieces. Using the above sample

sentences, there should be 25 pieces. (This step is important. If students do not have all 25 pieces, they cannot complete this task.)

5. Announce a set time limit of 10 minutes. Have the students work as quickly as possible to construct the sentences. Walk around the room and give hints to students who are having some difficulty. Obvious clues should be the capital letters and punctuation. However, the main focus here should be on gerund and infinitive combinations (e.g., *avoid + -ing, persuade + noun/pronoun + infinitive*).

Caveats and Options

1. Instead of having everyone work on the same set of sentences, prepare a half dozen envelopes. Each envelope should have several sentences cut into pieces. On the outside of each envelope, write (in large letters) a number on the envelope and the number of pieces inside (e.g., Envelope 4: 13 pieces). You will need more envelopes than pairs/groups.

   For example, if you have five groups, you will need about eight envelopes for this activity. Write the names of the pairs/groups on the board. Have each pair/group choose one envelope and begin working at the same time. When students have finished, they should raise their hands and the teacher should then check their work. If all of the sentences are correct, all of the pieces should be put back in the envelope. The teacher then writes that envelope number by the students' names on the board (because they have successfully completed that envelope). The students should then choose one of the remaining envelopes. This task can continue for a certain time limit set by the teacher or until one pair/group has finished with all of the envelopes.

   This alternative has a faster pace than the original exercise and is often more entertaining for the students. However, the advantage of the original exercise is that you can review all of the constructed sentences with all of the students very easily.

2. These activities are especially useful for review.

3. When practicing gerunds and infinitives, most grammar books use the traditional fill in the blanks (e.g., *Mark should avoid* _____

cigarettes.) The above activities offer an enjoyable way to practice the same grammar point.

Acknowledgments

A former teaching colleague, Beth Powell, showed me this idea.

Contributor

Keith S. Folse is the author of several ESL texts published by the University of Michigan Press.

Suggest for the Best

Levels
Intermediate +

Aims
Make accurate
statements with *suggest/
recommend/advise*,
stimulating production
through problem
solving and
identification with the
problem

Class Time
15–20 minutes

Preparation Time
5 minutes

Resources
Chalkboard or overhead
projector (OHP)

Verb complements with *suggest, recommend, advise* and the like are practiced, based on problem situations as illustrated in pictures.

Procedure

1. Before beginning the activity, draw three simple pictures on the board. These illustrations should depict problems with many solution. Some suggestions:

118

2. Go over the content of the pictures with the class, briefly describing the problems.
3. Put students into groups of three. Each group should discuss the problem and possible solutions, ultimately producing one sentence for each picture. Each sentence should use one of the following advice words: *recommend, suggest, advise.* No word should be used more than once so that each group produces one sentence practicing each word.
4. Put a model sentence on the board for each word (but not necessarily for the problems pictured on the board—a fourth picture-problem would be better).
5. Remind students that each group needs to produce only three sentences in all.
6. If the class is small, all advice sentences can be written on the board under the pictures. For a larger class, some can be written on the board; others can be spoken aloud to the whole class. It can also be done as a writing exercise to be turned in.

Possible models:

We advise him to call a doctor.

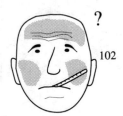

102

We suggest that he stay in bed.
We recommend that he take some medicine.

Caveats and Options

1. Three problems and three advice words are a simple and workable number. However, for a more lively or productive class, more pictures, more advice words, or a more demanding task (more than one sentence per picture) are advisable.
2. Other advice words: *urge, encourage, insist, demand, order*.
3. Although this activity in its raw form seems very simple, a profusion of correct versions of these patterns are extremely helpful for student mastery of this set of verbs, which are not identical in the range of grammatical patterns they allow.

Contributor

Victoria Holder teaches ESL at San Francisco State University and San Francisco City College, California, in the United States.

Gerunds and Infinitives Tic-Tac-Toe

Procedure

Levels
Intermediate

Aims
Practice using gerunds
and infinitives

Class Time
15 minutes/game

Preparation Time
5 minutes

Resources
List of verbs that take
gerunds, infinitives, or
both

1. For each game, prepare nine verbs from the list students have studied.
2. Introduce students to Tic-Tac-Toe by playing a simple game with a student in front of the class.
3. Divide the class into two teams.
4. Draw a Tic-Tac-Toe board on the chalkboard and in each square write a verb from your list; number the squares.
5. Flip a coin to determine which team starts; that team chooses a square. Then decide which student will give the correct responses.
6. After 20 seconds, the student must tell the instructor which classification the verb falls under, that is Group 1 (infinitives only), 2 (gerunds only), or 3 (both). Keep the list on the board as reinforcement.
7. The student gives a complete—and correct—sentence using the verb and the gerund or infinitive; the sentence should be a common one in spoken English.
8. If both answers are correct (to Steps 6 and 7), the student's team gets the square (X or O); if either answer is incorrect, the square is still free.
9. The other team has a turn until one team wins.
10. Give out prizes.

Caveats and Options

1. This is a game that can easily be modified and elaborated. You might require that sentences be complex, that two verbs be included in a single square, and so on. Also, a competition among classes can generate a great deal of interest in studying gerunds and infinitives.
2. With a little imagination, Tic-Tac-Toe games can be applied to other grammar points such as adverb or adjective clauses.

Contributor

Jeffrey Klausman is Instructor and Academic Adviser at the American Language Academy in Portland, Oregon, in the United States.

Picture This: Gerunds and Infinitives

Levels
Intermediate +

Aims
Review verbs that take infinitives to show unfulfilled propositions and verbs that take gerunds to show fulfilled propositions
Practice suprasegmental rhythm with each verb form to aid in its retention

Class Time
Several weeks

Preparation Time
Several hours

Resources
Grammar references (see References and Further Reading)

This activity helps students learn to associate gerunds and infinitives correctly with certain verbs through use of pictures.

Procedure

1. Create a set of pictures, each of which represents a single verb followed by its appropriate gerund or infinitive form. For example, a picture of two old ladies standing at the front door holding a gift in their hands could represent the sentence *They promised to bring a present* or the phrase *promise to bring*.
2. Present the generalization that infinitives show unfulfilled actions and underscore the DA-de-DA rhythm of infinitive structures.
3. Working only with the infinitive pictures, select one and repeat the sentence associated with it, for example, *They promised to bring a present*.
4. Show four more pictures in the same way, and then hold up the first picture until someone repeats the correct sentence or phrase. Work with five pictures at a time.
5. The next day, review the pictures already learned without saying anything (unless absolutely no one can remember the associated phrase).
6. Continue this until all of the infinitive pictures are learned.
7. Present the generalization that gerunds show fulfilled actions and underscore the DA-DE-da rhythm of gerund structures.
8. Working only with the gerund pictures, select one and repeat the sentence that is associated with it, for example, *He enjoys smoking cigarettes*.
9. Repeat the pattern until all the gerund pictures have been presented.

10. Now mix all the pictures together and practice with the class by simply holding up the picture.
11. Provide an exercise in which the students must select the gerund or infinitive form. The exercise should use the same words that were used with the pictures.
12. Provide a different exercise in which new verbs occur after the gerunds and infinitives.
13. Consolidate the exercise by asking students to describe themselves to another person (e.g., *I enjoy going to movies*) and to describe what they hope to do in the next 10 years (e.g., *I plan to get my MA degree*), either orally or in writing.

Caveats and Options

1. If the proficiency level of the group is not very high, reduce the number of pictures that are used and make sure that there is a close fit between the picture and the sentence or phrase that is associated with it.
2. Let the students themselves hold up the pictures for each other.
3. Using other magazine pictures, ask students to create a different sentence using the same main verb, for example, *John promised to water the garden* or *She enjoys fishing*, to encourage them to generalize from the example they have learned.
4. In an informal study, students tested 6 weeks later showed high retention of the patterns, for example, *promise to bring* and *enjoy smoking* simply by being shown the picture. This suggests that pictorial memory aids in the development of long-term memory traces.

References and Further Reading

Celce-Murcia, M., & Larsen-Freeman, D. (1983). *The grammar book.* Cambridge, MA: Newbury House.

Frank, M. (1972). *Modern English: A practical reference guide*. Englewood Cliffs, NJ: Prentice Hall.

Contributor

Peter Master is Associate Professor in the Department of Linguistics, California State University, Fresno, California, in the United States.

Part VI: Passive Voice and Ergative Verbs

Emma Has an Enemy

Levels
Intermediate

Aims
Contrast active and passive forms of ergative verbs while focusing on a known or suspected agent

Class Time
40 minutes–1 hour

Preparation Time
15 minutes

Resources
Copies of diary entries

Students compare active and passive forms of ergative verbs in different contexts.

Procedure

1. Present the class with the two diary entries below (or two similar entries of your own invention).

   > Dear Diary,
   > Maybe I'm paranoid, but I'm sure somebody's out to get me. On my way to work, as I was walking to the bus, a pile of bricks was dropped right in my path. They missed me by less than an inch! Then, when I got to the office, I noticed all the pens in my desk drawer had been broken in half, and all the letters I typed yesterday had been ripped to shreds. To top it all off, when I got home I found the windows in my flat had been shattered and my cat had been killed. I've never hurt anybody. I can't imagine who could be doing this to me.

   > Dear Diary,
   > What an unlucky day! It all started this morning at breakfast when my toast burned. Then my car broke down on the way to work. As I was trying to push it, my dress tore. I finally got to work, but during lunch a waitress carrying a heavy tray tripped, and iced tea spilled all over me. Later in the afternoon, my landlord called my office to tell me my pipes had burst and my whole apartment was flooded. To top it all off, when I finally got home, I found my cat had died! I sure hope I have better luck tomorrow.

2. Elicit information from students about the two characters. Ask if they can suggest reasons why such terrible things have been happening to the characters and what advice they would give them.
3. Have students work in pairs. Ask them to underline the verbs and identify the difference between the verbs in the two passages.

   Then have them list the verbs and try to identify a meaning component that they all have in common. Finally, ask them to try to change the active voice verbs into the passive voice and visa versa, and to

127

determine if the sentences still make sense or if the meaning changes with the change in voice.

4. Divide the class into two groups. Tell one group to imagine that somebody is "out to get them" and to write a diary entry about the bad things that have happened to them, using Emma's diary as a model. Tell the other group to imagine that they have been having bad luck and to write a similar diary entry to Bonnie's. Tell them to choose the verbs for their diary entries from the list below.

bend	bleach	break	burn	burst
change	crash	close	crack	drown
dry	empty	end	fade	shatter
shrink	shut	split	spread	stop

5. Have students exchange papers and see if they can change the verbs from passive to active or active to passive.
6. Ask the students if they can formulate a rule about when to use the active voice and when to use the passive voice with the above verbs. Elicit sample sentences.

Caveats and Options

1. The text can be adapted for all levels by adjusting the difficulty of the lexicon.
2. The same situation can be used for a role play: One character believes somebody is out to get them, and their partner tries to convince them that they're just having bad luck.

Contributor

Rodney Jones is University Assistant Lecturer in the English Department of the City Polytechnic of Hong Kong.

Doers and Causers

Levels
Intermediate

Aims
Review the use of
passive voice in process
descriptions while
learning the notion of
ergativity and ergative
verb

Class Time
1 hour

Preparation Time
1 hour

Resources
One short text
describing a
manufacturing process
One short text
describing a natural
process
Two diagrams relating
to the texts on an
overhead transparency
or chalkboard
Olives and a bottle of
olive oil (optional)

By comparing two texts, students learn the difference between ergative and nonergative verbs and the restrictions on passive voice related to this distinction.

Procedure

1. (Optional) Show students the olive oil and olives and elicit what they know about how olive oil is produced.
2. Show Diagram 1 (below). Explain to the students that the stages in the process are out of order and that they should listen to the text you are going to read to determine the correct order of the stages.

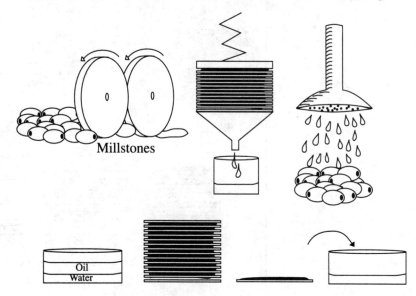

Millstones

Oil
Water

3. Read Text 1.

How Olive Oil is Made

The olives are first washed in water and then they are crushed under millstones. The resulting paste is spread on to mats. The mats are stacked up to fifty at a time and pressed under 300 to 400 tons of pressure. The resulting liquid contains oil and water. It is put into tanks and left to settle. The oil rises to the surface.

4. If necessary, have students discuss answers in pairs or groups.
5. Show Diagram 1b (below) and read text again.

1. are washed   2. _____   3. _____

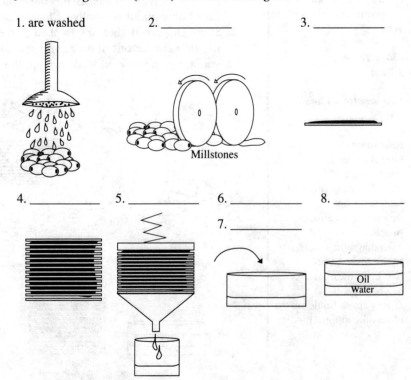

4. _____   5. _____   6. _____   8. _____

7. _____

6. Fill in verb form for Stage 1 (*are washed*) and instruct students to listen for and write down the verb forms for each of the later stages.
7. Read the text again.
8. Check students' answers (read text again if necessary), and fill in correct forms on the diagram. Draw students' attention to the deletion of *they are* after *and then* in Sentence 3, and of *it is* after *and* in Sentence 5.
9. Go around the class asking individual students to orally reconstruct as much as they can of the description of the process using Diagram 1 and the verb forms as prompts.
10. Elicit from students any knowledge they have about how rain comes about.
11. Read Text 2 and show Diagram 2.

The Rain Cycle

Water evaporates from seas, rivers and lakes and rises into the air as vapor. As the vapor cools, it condenses into droplets around tiny particles of dust, smoke and salt. It then falls as rain.

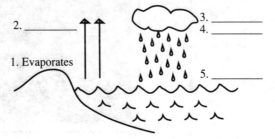

12. Fill in verb form for Stage 1 (*evaporates*) and instruct students to listen for and write down the verb forms for each of the later stages.
13. Check students' answers and fill in the correct forms on the diagram.

14. If there is time, go around the class asking individual students to orally reconstruct as much as they can of the description of the process, using Diagram 2 and the verb forms as prompts.

15. Ask students to discuss in pairs or groups why the verb forms differ between the two texts. They should be able (perhaps with some prompting) to come up with answers along the lines that Text 1 is a manufacturing process—a process carried out by people or machines—and the verb forms representing each stage in the process (apart from the last) imply a "doer" or "causer," whereas Text 2 is a natural process—a process in which events happen naturally—and the verb forms at each stage in the process do not imply any doer or causer.

16. Explain that some verbs in English can be used in both ways, depending on whether the event is seen as having a doer/causer or not. Some other verbs can only be used in one of the patterns.

On overhead transparency or chalkboard:

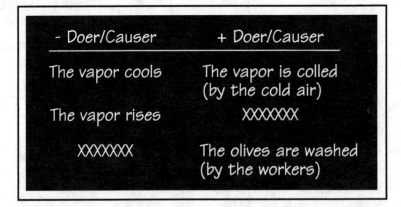

- Doer/Causer	+ Doer/Causer
The vapor cools	The vapor is colled (by the cold air)
The vapor rises	XXXXXXX
XXXXXXX	The olives are washed (by the workers)

Homework

Give the following list of verbs to the students and ask them to use dictionaries and grammar books to discover which of the verbs can be used in which of the patterns. In cases of verbs that can be used in both patterns, they should find or construct example sentences.

drop	fall	raise	press	condense
slip	develop	push	break	evaporate

Note that the students will need to be guided toward dictionaries that give sufficient examples and/or grammatical information to allow them to do this. Note also that the *Collins Cobuild English Language Dictionary* marks as *erg.* those verbs which can be used in both patterns. It may therefore be worth familiarizing students with the term *ergative*: Ergative verbs are verbs whose subjects in the active voice an be either the causer of the action or the thing affected by the action. Similarly, the *Collins Cobuild English Grammar* contains lists of ergative verbs.

Caveats and Options

Additional tasks can be assigned that require students to select appropriate verb forms in context by deciding whether the events should be represented as implying a doer/causer or not. The author has noted that one context in which students can have difficulty is that of the description of economic trends (e.g., *The economy developed rapidly in the early 1960s* or *The economy was developed rapidly in the early 1960s; Prices rose sharply last month* or *Prices were raised sharply last month*).

Contributor

Graham Lock is University Lecturer in the Department of English, City Polytechnic of Hong Kong.

Process Passives

Levels
Low
intermediate–intermediate

Aims
Use the passive form in
a process description

Class Time
30 minutes

Preparation Time
30 minutes

Resources
Copy of a process
description that also has
extra information in the
form of a narrative (see
Appendix)
Paper and colored
pencils
Transparency of text,
colored pens, and
overhead projector
(OHP).

S tudents learn to recognize the grammar of passive constructions in a series of activities involving highlighting, color coding, and drawing.

Procedure

1. Make enough copies of a process description text without the title for every student to have one.
2. Hand out the text and ask the students to read it and make suggestions for a suitable title. Write the titles on the board and get the class to choose the one they like best.
3. Show the class the text on the OHP. With a red pen, draw a box around the first noun of the process description, for example,

Trees are felled in the forest.

   Tell the class to look at their text and to draw a red box around all the words that do the same job as "Trees" in the sample sentence (the class may need more than one example).

4. Go around the class asking students to identify words that should have a red box around them on the transparency. Draw a red box around all the words they suggest.
5. Now draw a blue box around the verb form in the example sentence, for example,

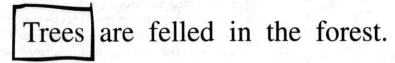

Trees are felled in the forest.

134

Ask the students to look at their texts and draw blue boxes around all similar types of words.

6. Repeat procedure as in Step 4. Identify all the verb forms on the transparency.
7. Now draw a green box around the complement in the example sentence, for example,

Trees are felled in the forest.

Students follow the same procedure as above, identifying all of the complements by drawing green boxes around them.

8. Now take a black pen and draw a box around the complete process description sentence, for example,

Trees are felled in the forest.

Ask the students to do the same with all the sentences they have identified.
9. Once the students have identified the process description from the narrative padding, ask them to draw simple pictures to illustrate the process described. If the students have a problem in drawing some of the sentences as pictures, then deal with vocabulary at this point (see Nation, 1994).
10. Once the passive has been introduced in the way outlined, the students can then be given a topic, such as, how a table is made, how a shirt is made. Working in groups, they first draw a series of pictures to show the process, then they write the description. Each group can have a different process to describe. Afterwards, they can change groups, show the pictures to the members of another group, and read them the description.

Caveats and Options

The passive is a very difficult structure for ESL students to use well. I have found that by taking the focus off the grammatical form and putting it onto the stages of the process, getting the students to identify the grammatical category of words needed to show a process, the students end up producing good process descriptions.

References and Further Reading

Nation, P. (Ed.). (1994). *New ways in teaching vocabulary.* Alexandria, VA: TESOL.

Appendix: Sample Text

Last year I went to Canada for my holidays. It is a wonderful country with lots to do and see. I took some organized tours while there and not only enjoyed myself but learned something too. One of my trips was to a paper mill to see paper being made. First, *trees are felled in the forest*. This happens not too far from the mill. *The branches and leaves are removed* before *the trees are transported to the sawmill*. It didn't take too many people to do all this, as machines do most of the work. We followed the trees to the sawmill, where *the bark is stripped from the trunks* . . .

Note: The process description is highlighted, while the rest of the text is narrative padding.

Acknowledgments

I first learned something similar to this technique from Pat McEldowney at Manchester University.

Contributor

Lindsay Miller is University Lecturer in the English Department, City Polytechnic of Hong Kong.

Introducing the Passive
With Rods

Levels
Intermediate

Aims
Learn the form and the function of the passive
Learn through illustration rather than explanation

Class Time
20 minutes

Preparation Time
5 minutes

Resources
Cuisenaire rods

Functional use of the passive can be introduced and practiced by setting up and acting out a scene using cuisenaire rods, pictures, or the students themselves.

Procedure

1. Use cuisenaire rods to set a scene that features a dog following a policeman following a mugger following a little old lady. The students can be expected to know all the words, with the possible exception of the word *mugger*.

2. Begin by asking a series of questions that cue the answers and make the action chain clear:

   What is the little old lady doing?
   (She is) walking . . .
   What is the mugger doing?
   (He is) following her . . .
   What is the policeman doing?
   (He is) following the mugger . . .
   What is the dog doing?
   (It is) following the policeman.
   (It is normal for a speaker to skip the words in parentheses.)

3. Continue with similar line of questions but now from a slightly different perspective:

   What is happening to the little old lady?
   She is being followed/chased/ . . .
   What is happening to the mugger?
   He is being followed/chased/ . . .

What is happening to the policeman?
He is being followed/chased/ . . .
What is happening to the dog?
Nothing.

If the students are having trouble with the form, the answers can be written on the board one sentence above another to help them out.

4. The last step is to switch back and forth between the two series of questions, producing active or passive answers depending upon the perspective taken in the question:

What is the mugger doing?
(He is) following the little old lady.
What is happening to the mugger?
He is being following/chased/ . . .
What is happening to the little old lady?
She is being chased/followed/ . . .
What is the little old lady doing?
(She is) walking/ . . .

Caveats and Options

1. Without too much work, it is possible to develop your own chain of events with which to illustrate the passive. All that is necessary is a string of related events, preferably involving three or four characters so that the chain is not too short.
2. This activity is designed to introduce the passive. It is meaningful, but not communicative as it is unquestionably teacher centered. In at least some senses, it is a disguised drill.
3. However, the activity provides a way to effectively illustrate something that is difficult to explain effectively.

Contributor

Graham Thurgood is Professor of Linguistics at California State University, Fresno, in the United States.

Having a Ball With Passive Verbs

Levels
Beginning–intermediate

Aims
Work on the active/
passive distinction with
visual and kinesthetic
reinforcement

Class Time
10–20 minutes

Preparation Time
10–15 minutes

Resources
Ball, cards, and tape

Practice with the passive voice grows naturally out of an activity in which students throw a ball to each other while describing their actions and the subsequent results.

Procedure

1. Throw the ball to a student, saying, "I threw the ball to [Mario]."
2. Gesture for Mario to throw the ball (gently) to another student. When he does this say, "[Mario] threw the ball to [Teng]." (Or elicit this sentence from the class.)
3. Tape up cards on board in order:

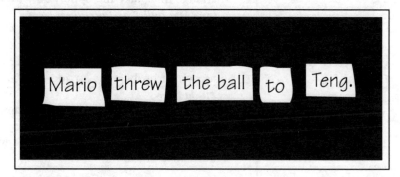

4. Gesture for Teng to throw the ball to another student. When he does this, say, "The ball was thrown by [Teng] to [Sylvie]."
5. Teach or review the rules and steps for changing active to passive, for example, the active subject X becomes the passive $by + X$. Rearrange positions of cards and add/subtract cards so that you have:

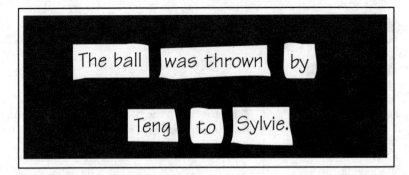

6. Have students continue to throw the ball and say either active or passive sentences. You or other students can rearrange the cards as necessary, either as prompts or as corrections.

7. Because transitive/intransitive distinctions are confusing, and students often try to make intransitive verbs passive, for example, *It was occurred*, when the ball falls on the floor at some point (you can arrange this), take the opportunity to say and review, "The ball fell." not *The ball was fall/fallen by X.*

Caveats and Options

1. I have also asked Japanese students to make paper origami balls for us, which enables me to add, *Kyoko made the ball. The ball was made by Kyoko.*

2. One approach is to start with a grammar lesson and try to find an appropriate illustrative object. However, it is sometimes more fruitful to start with an object and try to see what possible lessons could be developed around it.

Contributor

Lise Winer is Associate Professor in the Department of Linguistics, Southern Illinois University, in the United States.

Part VII: Adverbs and Adverbial Clauses

Professional Extremes

Levels
Intermediate +

Aims
Produce sentences with
result clauses while
stimulating production
through humor and
guessing

Class Time
25 minutes

Preparation Time
None

Resources
Chalkboard or overhead
projector (OHP)

Students guess people's jobs or professions based on statements made by other students that describe some aspect of their work in a result clause.

Procedure

1. As a class, brainstorm jobs and professions, writing them all on the board (at least 20).
2. Also as a class, brainstorm adjectives that could describe people in at least two of the professions or jobs. In other words, no adjective should be applicable to only one profession—each should be as versatile as possible. For example:

Profession:

hairdresser	typist	scientist
businessman	secretary	singer
bus driver	professor	salesclerk
mechanic	lawyer	doctor
nurse	judge	thief
bank teller	musician	firefighter
bank robber	carpenter	plumber

Adjectives:

fat	thin	tall	stupid
old	smart	talented	loud
rich	fast	intelligent	careful
good	honest	dishonest	strong
bad	strict	polite	clever

143

3. Pair off students. Each pair should try to make one (or more) sentences in which they match one adjective with one profession—but they do not actually mention the profession—according to the pattern *so* + adj. + *that* clause.

   The purpose is to make a sentence that allows the rest of the class to guess the job or profession of the subject of the sentence.

   Example:

   > He's so careful that his cash drawer is always correct at the end of the day.
   > Answer: Bank teller

4. Give a few more examples for the class to guess. Write them on the board. The more examples that you give, the more easily and enthusiastically the students will fall into the activity.

   More Examples:

   > He is so loud that people can hear him in the last row of the highest balcony in the theater.
   > Answer: Singer

   > He is so talented that he can play seven different instruments.
   > Answer: Musician

   > He is so polite that his regular passengers bring him presents for Christmas.
   > Answer: Bus driver

5. Have each pair of students present their sentence(s) to the class for guessing.

Caveats and Options

1. This could be done as a whole-class activity to save time, but in that case, students who are shy are less likely to participate. It could also be done in groups, with the guessing taking place within the group, but then it is more difficult to monitor accuracy unless something is submitted in writing.

2. Alternatively, this format could be used to practice adverbs—*He drives so carelessly that his passengers always fall on the floor*—by brainstorming either verbs (e.g., *drives*, *types*) or adverbs instead of adjectives.

Contributor

Victoria Holder teaches ESL at San Francisco State University and San Francisco City College, California, in the United States.

What Do You Think of My Hero/Heroine?

Levels
Beginning; secondary +

Aims
Increase students' repertoire of intensifier adverbs and help them recognize the degree of intensity of adverbs

Class Time
50 minutes

Preparation Time
1 hour

Resources
A two to three page short story entitled *My Hero/Heroine* written as a homework assignment or in a previous class by each student on a person of their choice
A list of intensifier adverbs brainstormed by the whole class

Students are introduced to adverbs that serve as intensifiers or downtoners; for example, *fairly courageous, incredibly stupid, pretty convincing, terribly self-centered, rather introverted*, based on a three-page story entitled *My Hero/Heroine* that they have already written.

Procedure

1. Students bring to class a three-page short story entitled *My Hero/ Heroine* which they have individually written at home.
2. Write two adverbs, each followed by an adjective, on the board to demonstrate their varying degree of intensity. For example, you can ask students: "Comparing *fairly courageous* and *extremely courageous*, which adverb is more intense?" "Comparing *rather stupid* and *very stupid*, which adverb is less intense?"
3. The teacher asks students to brainstorm as many adverbs showing intensity as possible and then categorize them into three levels, low, medium, and high. For example:

High	*Medium*	*Low*
incredibly	rather	fairly
extraordinarily	quite	mildly
significantly	clearly	vaguely
amazingly	surprisingly	interestingly

4. Check that all these brainstormed adverbs are properly categorized.
5. If necessary, you could supply extra examples from a supplementary list.
6. Students then pair off.
7. Students in each pair read each other's story for 10 minutes.

8. One of the students in a pair asks, "What do you think of my hero/ heroine, and why?" while the other student responds by using any of the suggested intensifier adverbs. (Refer to the examples below for sample responses. For more advanced learners, they could be encouraged to supply their own intensifiers.)
9. Students exchange roles and repeat Step 8.

More examples:
I think your hero is *rather* irrational throughout the story because he . . .
I think your heroine is *too* good to be true because . . .
I find your hero *quite* amusing because . . .
I am *utterly* confused by the character development of your heroine because . . .

Caveats and Options

1. You can walk around the classroom to supervise the discussions.
2. Whenever you hear a wrong part of speech given as an intensifier, as in *fair* for *fairly*, you should point out the error to the student.
3. Instead of asking about the hero or heroine, students could also ask each other what they think about the story in their discussion.
4. As a follow-up activity, each pair could write up a journal entry reflecting on the most useful intensifier adverbs to them.

Contributor

Patrick Ng is University Assistant Lecturer in the Department of English of the City Polytechnic of Hong Kong.

Colorless Green Ideas Sleep Furiously

Levels
Intermediate +

Aims
Generate adverbs of manner in an imaginative framework to practice their use and placement

Class Time
30–50 minutes

Preparation Time
Enough to gather some newspapers

Resources
Newspapers

This activity practices adverbs of manner in a creative and whimsical way.

Procedure

1. On the board write, "Colorless green ideas sleep *furiously*," underlining or otherwise highlighting (e.g., by use of a different color chalk or marker) the manner adverb.
2. Explain that although this sentence makes no sense, it was made famous by the linguist Noam Chomsky as an example of a meaningless but grammatical sentence.
3. Tell students that an "ad-verb" is added to a verb to modify or elaborate its meaning in some way, as in:

sleep *furiously*   glowed *brightly*
Verb Adverb   Verb Adverb

Many adverbs can be made by adding *-ly* to an adjective, as in these examples. These adverbs answer the question How? of the verb:

How did the ideas sleep? *Furiously.*
How did her eyes glow? *Brightly.*

4. Ask students to brainstorm some adjectives, for example: *strange, quiet, happy.*
5. Then have them make manner adverbs with the adjectives to fit into the anomalous sentence on the board, for example:

Colorless green ideas sleep strangely, quietly, happily . . . .

Mention that final *-y* becomes *i* before *-ly.*

6. Put students in pairs or small groups and give out a page of a newspaper or a whole newspaper to each pair/group.
7. Tell students they are to select two to three suitable short headlines—they must contain a verb—and then to add various adverbs of manner to these to make grammatical sentences. For example:

> Oil Prices Rise *furiously, quietly* . . . .
> Man Bites Dog *ferociously, hungrily* . . . .

Encourage them to be imaginative.

8. Each group writes its headlines on the board, and the class votes on which altered headline(s) they like the best.

Caveats and Options

1. Note that many adverbs—for example, those describing intrinsic qualities such as old, young, tall, color words—cannot occur in the *-ly* form.
2. The activity can be expanded beyond a focus on adverbs by allowing students to add any elements they wish—for example, adjectives (i.e., adjective phrases)—to the original headlines to make expanded headlines. The other students then try to guess which part of the expanded headline is the original headline.

References and Further Reading

Chomsky, N. (1957). *Syntactic structures*. The Hague: Mouton.

Acknowledgments

Apologies to Noam Chomsky for using his sentence in a way he surely never intended.

Contributor

Martha C. Pennington is University Reader (Research Coordinator) in English at the City Polytechnic of Hong Kong.

Causal Signals

Levels
Intermediate +

Aims
Become aware of
different alternatives for
representing causal
relationships
Use signals of causal
relationships—verbs,
words, and phrases

Class Time
30 minutes

Preparation Time
15–30 minutes

Resources
One text set for each
group of five
An introductory
paragraph written on
the top of a piece of
cardboard
Handout (see
Appendix)

Learners' attention is drawn to signals of cause and effect by breaking up and jumbling texts to highlight their various grammatical forms.

Procedure

1. Choose four consecutive paragraphs from an expository text on causal relations.
2. Write the first paragraph on a large piece of cardboard as introduction.
3. Jumble the second, third and fourth paragraphs and put each bit on a small piece of paper as follows:

   a. Write each causal signal on a small piece of paper.
   b. Break up the rest of the paragraphs by punctuation marks and write each bit ending with a punctuation mark on a small piece of paper.

4. Make enough sets of materials for the whole class.
5. With the class, brainstorm for signals of causal relations.
6. In pairs, learners refer to the handout and discuss the use of different types of signals: verbs, words, and phrases.
7. In groups, learners arrange three consecutive paragraphs on a cardboard, where an introductory paragraph is written on the top.
8. With the class, discuss the answers and accept alternatives wherever possible.

Caveats and Options

For smaller or faster classes:
1. All groups display their cardboard pieces and go round the room freely to select the best solution.

2. Each group takes a turn to justify their selection while the teacher acts as a facilitator and explains.
3. As a follow-up activity, the teacher may ask the learners to produce a short text of two or more paragraphs using the signals on the handout.
4. To make it fun, learners work in small groups and have a contest to see which group uses the most signals appropriately.

Appendix: Sample Handout

Signals of Causal Relations		
Verbs	Words/Phrases	
cause	in	as a result of
make . . . possible	hence	
affect	by	for this reason
	because of	
bring about	for	therefore
	otherwise	
produce	so	consequently
	as	
give reasons for	thus	accordingly
accomplish	since	on account of
originate	due to	owing to
follow from	because	by the agency of
make possible	if	by means of
result from	then	in effect

Contributor

Wai-king Tsang is University Lecturer in the Department of English, City Polytechnic of Hong Kong.

Part VIII: Questions and Answers

Question Rods

Levels
Beginning

Aims
Practice wh-questions
and answers by
visualizing and
manipulating sentence
patterns

Class Time
15 minutes

Preparation Time
10 minutes

Resources
Cuisenaire rods

Here is a beginning-level activity using cuisenaire rods to elicit and to illustrate the structure of simple wh-questions and answers.

Procedure

1. Cut out the elements of an information question and tape it to separate rods as illustrated below:

2. Cut out and tape the answer on the back of each corresponding rod from Step 1, as illustrated below:

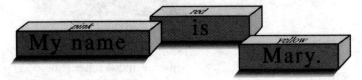

3. Fix several rods as in Steps 1 and 2 for small-group practice.
4. Put the rods down in order (see Step 1) and read the question aloud together with the students.
5. Show the answer by turning the rods over and putting them in the new, correct order (see Step 2).
6. Let some of the students repeat Steps 4 and 5.
7. Once Step 6 is done successfully, students should work in small groups with their own rods.

Caveats and Options

1. When students can do Step 7 successfully, there are a variety of ways to expand this activity. Just be sure to use the same sentence patterns.

155

Below are some suggestions that can be followed in sequence, but don't feel limited; listening to your students is best.

a. Students use their own names in the answer; they should turn the yellow rod on a side that has no information taped to it.

b. Students add their own information to the question. They may ask: *What are your names?* (to two students). Again, they have the freedom to do this by turning the red and pink rods on the blank sides.

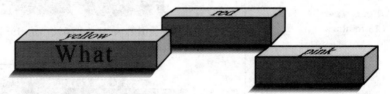

c. Students change additional information in either the question or answer; the teacher should encourage this. For example, the question might be: *What is on your desk?* (yellow rod on blank side). The answer could be: *The book is on my desk.* (pink and yellow rods on blank sides). In both cases, the same sentence structures are being reinforced.

2. Other alternatives include:

   Different question types: who, where, how many, yes/no questions
   Verb tenses
   Modal auxiliaries
   Tag questions

3. This exercise can be used to visualize and manipulate structures and grammar points as a presentation, practice, or review. However, it mainly gives students the freedom to practice and expand upon the information, based on their own interests and abilities.

Contributor

Lauren Alderfer is a high school English teacher at the Academia Cotopaxi in Quito, Ecuador.

Interview Circles

Levels
High beginning

Aims
Practice the interrogative form and respond to questions

Class Time
Varies

Preparation Time
30–40 minutes

Resources
Handout (see Appendix)

Students ask and answer yes/no questions in pairs arranged in concentric circles.

Procedure

1. Give the handout to everyone. Explain that they will form questions using the statements on it. Then break up the class into groups of 12-14, and have each group form dyads in two circles, with the same number in the inner and outer circles. Make sure that each student in the inner circle is in front of someone in the outer circle, forming a pair. The students in each pair need to face each other, as illustrated in the following sketch:

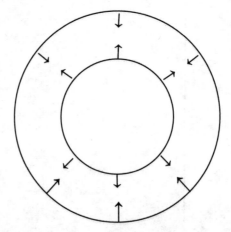

2. Explain that students are going to interview each other in order to learn about the other people in the class. The students ask and answer

with the person in front of them. The members of each pair take turns asking and answering questions, one question at a time. They can choose any question to ask, and they can ask as many questions as they like within a given time period. The interviewer lists the student's response in either the Yes or No column. The students need to get at least one name for each question. The interview time per pair can be varied, from 1 to 3 minutes, and students can be encouraged to add their own questions. An example of an interview question and response is the following:

Q: Do you like outdoor activities?
A: Yes, I like outdoor activities.
      or
    No, I don't like outdoor activities.

Students can be required to respond in a full sentence for practicing the affirmative and negative forms.

3. To start the activity, tell the students in the outer circle to ask a question.
4. Clap your hands after 3 minutes, and tell those in the inner circle to move to their right so as to face the next person in the outer circle. Have them repeat this movement until they finish rotating one round.
5. Tell the students to form one big circle. Then ask them what names they got for the questions. For example, you will ask: "Who likes outdoor activities?" As students raise their hands to be recognized, call on one who might answer: *Kumiko likes outdoor activities.*

   Then ask: "Who doesn't like outdoor activities?" and so forth. You may require the students to answer in a full sentence.

Caveats and Options

1. Students at the beginning level are often hesitant about speaking because of their limited vocabulary and ability to make grammatical sentences. This activity will give them an opportunity to speak on a limited basis, and they will gradually become more confident about speaking.

2. Moskowitz (1978) says that if the learners get to know each other through the process of giving and receiving information about themselves, warmth and closeness develop; and having a healthy relationships with others is conducive to learning.

References and Further Reading

Moskowitz, C. (1978). *Caring and sharing in the foreign language class.* Boston: Heinle & Heinle.

Appendix: Sample Handout

Search for someone who . . .	Names	Yes	No
1. likes outdoor activities.	_____	____	____
2. plays the piano.	_____	____	____
3. listens to classical music every day.	_____	____	____
4. talks to plants.	_____	____	____
5. has a dog.	_____	____	____
6. has visited Paris more than once.	_____	____	____
7. saw Star Wars four times.	_____	____	____
8. went abroad last year.	_____	____	____
9. would like to be an astronaut.	_____	____	____
10. has owned a snake.	_____	____	____
11. has been to Africa.	_____	____	____
12. reads a book before going to bed.	_____	____	____

Adapted from Moskowitz (1978, p.52)

Contributor

Miyako Arakawa is a student at Temple University of Japan.

Press Conference

Levels
Intermediate +

Aims
Put into practice the
rules about reporting
what someone says
while using English in a
real-life situation

Class Time
1 hour and 20 minutes

Preparation Time
10 minutes

Resources
An article taken from a
local newspaper on a
topic controversial
enough to be the reason
for a press conference
Sticky labels or badges
to identify participants

Students participate in a simulated press conference to practice reported speech.

Procedure

1. Divide the class in half. Tell one half that they are going to be an interest group (e.g., Amnesty International) and will hold a press conference on the issue at hand. Assign individual roles if desired (e.g., Chairman). Tell them that they will be expected to open the press conference by stating their position on the issue and that they should then invite questions from the floor. Tell the other half that they are going to be journalists attending a press conference given by the interest group and that they will have an opportunity to ask questions. Have students write their name and role on a label and wear it.
2. Give out the newspaper clipping and ask students to read it.
3. Ask students to think about what they will say at the press conference, to formulate questions, and to anticipate what questions will be asked according to their roles. Tell the students that they will be expected to make brief notes on the important points raised (journalists) and the questions asked (interest group), as this information will form the basis of a writing activity later.
4. When all are sufficiently prepared, begin the press conference. If possible, arrange the seating in the class to simulate a press conference venue. Tell the interest group to begin by stating their position.
5. The conference should proceed with the journalists asking questions and members of the interest group answering until the allotted time is used up or until there are no more questions.
6. Students should then return to their original places to write.

7. Tell the journalists to write an article to appear on the front page of a local newspaper. Tell them to focus on what was said and by whom at the press conference.

8. Tell the interest group to write a short article for their newsletter reporting on the press conference. Tell them to concentrate on reporting the questions asked and the replies given.

Caveats and Options

1. A large class could be divided into four groups.

2. The nature of the writing could be changed, for example, into a personal letter for the interest group.

3. Students could write in pairs instead of on their own.

4. This could be a more controlled press conference if each participant were required to make a specific contribution, for example, to ask/answer at least one question.

5. The activity can be lengthened or shortened at all stages; it is very versatile.

6. Students could be asked to come up with their own topics and clippings and negotiate about which one should be the focus of the press conference.

7. You can make the activity more challenging by providing several clippings on the same topic. This would be easy to do for topics that are constantly in the news, for example, pollution. Although this would require more preparation, clippings could be used again and again.

8. This activity is particularly suitable for students who are studying professional English or who are not afraid to speak up in large groups. It is important to stress that you require certain kinds of information, that is, that which relates to what was said and by whom it was said. Otherwise, the students may be tempted to give general discussion of the press conference or the issue instead.

References and Further Reading

Adapted from "The Press Conference" in Ladousse, G. P. (1987). *Role play*. Oxford: Oxford University Press.

Contributor

Neil Drave is Lecturer in English in the College of Higher Vocational Studies at the City Polytechnic of Hong Kong.

Interest Survey

Levels
Intermediate +

Aims
Produce a variety of
questions and report
responses
Build group spirit and
cohesion while learning
about differing and
common interests

Class Time
Three 50-minute class
periods

Preparation Time
5–10 minutes

Students survey each other on a variety of topics as a way to work on questions and reported speech.

Procedure

1. Divide class into groups of four or five students and assign each group a topic (e.g., work, career goals, sports, music, movies, television, food, other interests).
2. Each group forms questions (one for each member of the group plus one) on its assigned topic to be used to survey all members of the class and then writes the questions on the board.
3. The whole class participates as you point to the questions. Students indicate any grammatical corrections that need to be made for each question and consider whether they would be willing to answer it.
4. Each group assigns one of its questions to each of its members (if the extra question has not been deleted, it can be discarded).
5. In the second class period, the teacher gives everyone a list of all the students in the class with space between each name. Students then survey each class member individually, asking the question assigned by the group.
6. For homework, students tally their results; for example, in response to the question, "What is your favorite kind of ethnic food?", the results might be, *Six students responded that their favorite was Chinese food, three Japanese, one Korean, one Russian, one Pakistani.*
7. In the next class period, students report the results of their survey question to their group. Each group then gives a report of their findings to the whole class.

Caveats and Options

1. The focus of the activity can be varied—either questions or reported speech.
2. If writing practice is desired, either you or the groups can make up sheets containing the questions for each topic, for example, a food sheet or a sports sheet, with a space below each question for students to fill in their answers. Copies can then be made for all of the students (or, in a large class, half the students could do some of the topics and the other half the remaining topics). The students can then fill in the answers for homework. During the next class period, each group is responsible for collecting all the sheets on its assigned topic, tallying the results, and reporting them to the class.

Contributor

Margaret Grant teaches in the ESL program at San Francisco State University, California, in the United States.

Group Newspapers

Levels
Beginning–intermediate

Aims
Develop skill in asking
and answering wh-
questions in context

Class Time
50-60 minutes

Preparation Time
15–30 minutes

Resources
Any grammar text
Newspaper articles

A newspaper format motivates students to try to reconstruct information in a story by means of wh-questions.

Procedure

1. Write a short paragraph on the board. Format it as a newspaper article.
2. Ask students to list important information provided in the paragraph.
3. As students retell information points, erase them from the story.
4. Ask students wh-questions to elicit the necessary information. Write the questions on the board as they are asked. Have students take turns completing the missing portions of the article, as other students answer the wh-questions.

Caveats and Options

1. Underline the information items. Have students provide wh-questions for these instead of reconstructing the story.
2. Ask wh-questions from the outset and create a story from students' answers.
3. Create several sections of a newspaper on board. Provide different information for different types of articles.
4. Put the story in the present tense. Ask questions in the past tense. Change the story on the board to the past tense as questions are answered.
5. Separate class into groups, giving each a short newspaper article. They create wh-questions to ask of the next group in order to find out the contents of the next group's articles. Students can also create their own stories on this model.

6. This exercise can highlight different verb tenses. You can write several stories on large white sheets of paper for reuse.
7. Use an overhead projector if available.

Contributor

Virginia Martin teaches ESL in the English Department, Bowling Green State University, Ohio, in the United States.

Riddle in the Middle

Levels
Intermediate

Aims
Produce a variety of
yes/no questions and
short responses,
stimulating production
through curiosity,
humor, and gamelike
features

Class Time
30 minutes

Preparation Time
10 minutes

Resources
Riddles (see References
and Further Reading)

While seated in a circle, students practice questions and short answers using humorous material.

Procedure

1. Make a list of enough riddles for every student to have one. (See Appendix for samples.)
2. Cut the list into strips to make individual ones.
3. Put students into a circle with one student in the middle, either standing or sitting.
4. The student in the middle states his or her riddle ("What's black and white and read all over?"), then selects another student to begin trying to guess the riddles.
5. Going around the circle, each student asks yes/no question to try to guess the riddle (*Is it a flag?*) or to get further information (*Can you eat it? Does it have more than four letters?*). Stand behind the circle and move around as needed to consult with any student who needs assistance in vocabulary, grammar, or pronunciation when asking a question.
6. The student in the middle answers with short responses (*No, it isn't. No, you can't. No, it doesn't.*).
7. The student who guesses the riddle moves to the middle position, or, if that student has already had a turn in the middle position, selects another student who has not yet been in the middle position. Then the procedure begins again, continuing until all students have had a turn in the middle of the circle.

Caveats and Options

1. If the group has more than 20 students, make two circles, each with a student in the middle; use a native-speaker aide or student helper, if available, with the second group.

2. Or, if the group has more than 20 students, make two concentric circles. The students in the inner circle ask the questions of the student in the middle, while those in the outer circle serve as their partners, each student in the outer circle being paired with one in the inner circle. The student in the outer circle is to assist his/her partner in formulating questions.
3. Use the same format for the Twenty Questions game.
4. This activity is best used to practice and expand students' repertoire of questions after they already have basic mastery of yes/no question and response patterns. It is a good way to spiral or review those patterns.

References and Further Reading

A good source for riddles is Clark, D. A. (1981). *The giant joke book.* New York: Doubleday.

Appendix: Sample Riddles

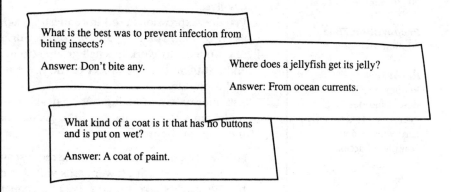

What is the best was to prevent infection from biting insects?

Answer: Don't bite any.

Where does a jellyfish get its jelly?

Answer: From ocean currents.

What kind of a coat is it that has no buttons and is put on wet?

Answer: A coat of paint.

Contributor

Martha Pennington is University Reader (Research Coordinator) in English at the City Polytechnic of Hong Kong.

Matching Requests

Levels
Beginning–intermediate

Aims
Practice requesting,
agreeing, and refusing
while developing
fluency within a
communicative
framework

Class Time
20–30 minutes

Preparation Time
30 minutes

Resources
Request cards
describing needs in
everyday life and reply
cards describing a
completed action.

Students are given an opportunity to practice request-grant/request-refusal adjacency pairs in the hope that by practicing basic functions repeatedly, students will be able to produce appropriate expressions fluently and spontaneously.

Procedure

1. Prepare 20–25 pairs of request and reply cards for each group. Request cards have a question mark "?" in the top right-hand corner, and reply cards have a tick (✔).
2. Ask students for situations in which they need help in their everyday lives.
3. Practice expressions used in requesting, agreeing, and refusing such as *Can/Could you . . . ?*; *Yes, of course; Sorry, I'm busy*, and so forth.
4. Ask students to work in small groups (four to five students in each), and tell them that the object of the game is the matching of request and reply cards.
5. Ask one student in each group to deal out five request cards and five reply cards to each player of the group, and then tell the students the rules of the game:

   a. The players who have matching request and reply cards can discard them. Players with fewer cards will be close to winning the game.
   b. The players take turns to make a request based on the cards in hand, and the request can be addressed to anyone in the group.
   c. When a player has a reply card that corresponds to the request, he or she gives it to the requester with an appropriate response and a comment on it. If he or she does not have such a card, he or she refuses the request with an appropriate response and tells the reason why he or she cannot help the requester.

d. The player who first completes the matching of all cards is the winner.

Caveats and Options

1. If the students are at the intermediate level, you may want to require them to make requests in formal and informal speech and to respond to them in an appropriate way.
2. This activity is designed so that students may participate in it without feeling threatened. A small-group game situation is employed in this activity so that students' affective filter is low.
3. Richards and Schmidt (1983) note that, in practicing request-grant adjacency pairs, many students tend to make short stilted responses that are likely to hinder the smooth flow of conversation. Therefore, L2 learners need to acquire some strategies to not only answer a question but also to give some extra information and then to ask another question in order to keep the conversation going on. Gatbonton and Segalowitz (1988) maintain that automaticity is promoted through repeatedly practicing the notions and functions of everyday life.

References and Further Reading

Gatbonton, E., & Segalowitz, N. (1988). Creative automatization: Principles for promoting fluency within a communicative framework. *TESOL Quarterly, 22,* 473-492.

Hadfield, J. (1985). *Elementary communication games: A collection of games and activities for elementary students of English.* Surry, England: Thomas Nelson.

Richards, J. C., & Schmidt, R. W. (1983). Conversational analysis. *Language and Communication* (pp. 117-154). London: Longman.

Contributor

Junko Sato is an ESL teacher enrolled in the Temple University of Japan MA in TESOL course.

Stand-Up Substitution Cards

Levels
Beginning–intermediate

Aims
Perceive a visual and tactile dimension to the practice of word order to "feel" syntactic changes occurring in question formation and negation

Class Time
7–10 minutes

Preparation Time
20–30 minutes

Resources
Heavy construction paper or cardboard, cut into large pieces
Wide felt-tip pens or markers of different colors

This activity gets learners out of their chairs and moving around the class, thus breaking the routine of a traditional grammar class, as they work on various aspects of sentence structure involving questions, negation, and statements.

Procedure

1. To practice the simple present tense, prepare color-coded cards as follows:

   pink   third person singular nouns, pronouns, verb endings, and auxiliary verbs
   purple   parts of speech for all other persons
   green   main verbs (roots, with no endings)
   yellow   adverbs, objects, prepositional phrases going after the main verb
   black   punctuation marks

   Write each word or verb ending on a separate card, writing large enough so the words can be read from the back of the class.

   A set of 15 cards for the simple present tense (positive, negative, and yes/no question forms) might consist of the following (a slash indicates that both sides of one card are used):

pink	*purple*	*green*	*yellow*	*black*
John	I	go/play	homework/late	?/.
She/she	You/you	do/sleep	to the sauna/soccer	
He/he	We/we	soccer		
s/es	They/they	s/es		
doesn't/Does		don't/Do		

172

2. Give each student a card, pointing out those cards inscribed on both front and back.

3. Call out a sentence composed of the above cards (e.g., *I sleep late.*)

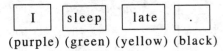

(purple) (green) (yellow) (black)

4. The students holding the cards called out (in this case four students— *I, sleep, late,* and *.*) go to the front of the class and hold up their cards in line, thus making a complete sentence that the rest of the class can see.

5. The whole class repeats the sentence in chorus.

6. The teacher then calls out another word (e.g., *he*), and the student holding the appropriate card takes his/her place in the sentence at the front of the class. If necessary, a student whose place is being taken should stand to the side. (In this case the student holding *he* will replace the student with *I* and the student with *s* should stand up next to *sleep,* thus agreeing with the new subject.)

7. The class again repeats the newly formed sentence aloud.

8. Continue calling out substitutions while students stand up, stand to the side, or switch positions with other students as necessary. Note that students with double-sided cards may simply have to turn over their card, and make sure sentences always start with a capital letter. Prompts such as *negative, positive, question,* and *sentence* (meaning *affirmative positive*) can be included.

9. Continually quicken the pace of substitutions as students catch on to the activity, and make sure that the students standing to the side are standing where they can see those who are making a sentence so that all may repeat each newly formed sentence in chorus.

Caveats and Options

1. If you have a large class, two students can be assigned one card, some students can just stay seated and help those substituting, or you can make more cards by using only one side of each card. If you have too few students, give more than one card to some of the students.

Here are some sample sets of cards for other structures:

Have to/has to (positive and negative forms)

purple	*red*	*yellow*	*brown*
I	He	has	to clean the house.
You	She	like	to go to the doctor.
We	doesn't		to play games.
They	s		to watch TV.
don't			
ve			

Going to future (+, -, y/n?, and wh? forms)

brown	*purple*	*red*	*orange*	*green*	*yellow*	*black*
What	I	am	not	going to	write a letter	?
You/you	Is/is				visit a friend	
He/he	Are/are				do	
She/she						
We/we						
They/they						

Simple past (passive and active forms)

yellow	*green*	*red*	*brown*
Leonardo da Vinci/	painted	was/were	The Mona Lisa
by Leonardo da Vinci	wrote/written		Romeo and Juliet/
William Shakespeare/			Julius Cesar and
by William Shakespeare			Romeo and Juliet

2. This activity can work either as a part of a presentation of a new grammar structure or as a way of reviewing the mechanics of a previously presented structure. It is best to keep the pace lively and stop the activity as soon as all the desired forms have been successfully drilled. As students become acquainted with the procedure, prompt less and less, even to the point of simply gesturing with the hands or

face. Contextualizing can transform this activity from a mechanical exercise to a more communicative one by using picture cues or situations to prompt.

Contributor

John Wheeler is Coordinator of the United States Information Agency EFL Fellows Program, Slovakia, based at the National Pedagogical Institute, in Bratislava.

Part IX: General Purpose Grammar Activities

Grammar Translation Line Up

Levels
Beginning +

Aims
Practice the quick and accurate production of important grammatical structures, functional chunks and vocabulary held in memory

Class Time
30 minutes

Preparation Time
10–15 minutes

Resources
Textbook and materials previously used during the term

In a game format, students match items from the L1 with translation equivalents in the L2.

Procedure

1. Before class, review the course syllabus and textbook, and choose examples of the key grammatical structures, functional chunks, and vocabulary that you want to review or test. Note down 20 or 25 phrases each containing one of these key elements that you want to review.
2. Pair off students, making sure that weaker students are paired with stronger students. Pairs should bring two chairs to the front of the room and sit so that one is facing the chalkboard and the other is facing his or her partner (facing away from the board). Pairs will now be lined up in two lines in front of and parallel to the chalkboard.
3. Write a phrase in English containing a key language element on the chalkboard. (Do not let students speak until you have finished writing). The students facing the board should quickly translate this phrase and tell it to their partners using the L1 only. The students with their backs to the board, on hearing the phrase spoken in the L1, have to guess what that phrase would be in English.
4. Whoever raises his or her hand first and tells you the phrase that you have on the board wins a point for the team. You may want to let every student have one guess before letting anyone have a second guess. You also need to decide if metatalk about the language (e.g., *No, in the past tense.*) is permissible. Keep track of the points and award a round of applause (at least) to the winners.

Caveats and Options

1. If you would rather avoid the competitive element that comes with having teams, you can have the pairs change regularly. The students will still enjoy this activity.
2. This activity is particularly useful with classes of false beginners who have previously studied grammar and reading and are now beginning to access this knowledge for use in communication.
3. This game works well on the last day of class, before a vacation, or during a class party.

Contributor

Eric Bray is Academic Director of the Kyoto YMCA English School, in Japan.

Communicative Tasks for Grammar Consciousness Raising

Levels
Intermediate

Aims
Learn grammar
structures through
communicative task
performance

Class Time
50-65 minutes

Preparation Time
1-2 hours

Resources
Grammar textbooks and
teacher references (see
References and Further
Reading)

These exercises offer meaning-focused use of the target language in which students perform communicative tasks that have a resolvable grammar problem as the task content.

Procedure

1. Select the grammar structure. This is best done by noting common errors in students' work. Because grammar tasks can be designed for most structures, they are also appropriate for those teachers who must follow a structural syllabus. However, the structure selected should be simple enough for students to learn through task performance. Grammar points such as adverb placement and indirect object placement are difficult for students, yet only require mastery of a few rules, whereas grammar points such as relative clause usage or article usage are governed by a great many rules. Tasks dealing with such grammar points should focus on only selected aspects of usage. (See relative clause task in Appendix B.)

2. Design the task sheet and task cards. Studies of task features show that the most communication is produced when the tasks have four components:

   a. They are multiway information gap tasks in which all students hold unique information that must be shared with others.
   b. They are tasks that allow students to plan what they will say, perhaps by modeling after a task sentence.
   c. They are tasks that require a solution.

d. They are tasks in which all students must reach agreement on the solution.

Vary these tasks, depending on the ability of the students. If the students are not used to task performance, give them a less demanding task, for example, one that is not an information gap task or that does not require a single, agreed-upon task solution. After students have become skilled at task performance, they can attempt tasks with all four features.

Two sample tasks are given in the Appendices: an adverb task, which is not an information gap task (so there are no task cards) but requires a task solution (Appendix A); and a relative clause task, which is an information gap task but does not require a solution (Appendix B).

3. Design the grammar test, basing it on the task sheet. The test should have an objective section (such as multiple choice or grammaticality judgment sentences) and a production section. The test for the relative clause task is given in Appendix C.

4. After developing the material, give students the pretest, which can be done the day before the lesson or directly before the task. After they complete their task sheet, they should take the posttest. Review the task sheet and test answers.

Caveats and Options

1. You may want to audiotape task performance and then give feedback to the groups on their performance, such as by writing the performance times on the board, praising language use, and so on.

2. This activity can be used as one component of a communicative lesson. For example, the students can perform a task on the structure, then go on to a number of communicative activities that contain the grammar structure.

3. Through communicative exposure to grammar structures in task performance, students will be able to consolidate their knowledge and be more apt to acquire the structure.

4. Teachers working from more traditional material can use the task to add a communicative activity to their formal presentation of grammatical material.

References and Further Reading

Celce-Murcia, M., & Larsen-Freeman, D. (1983). *The grammar book*. Cambridge, MA: Newbury House.

Fotos, S., & Ellis, R. (1991). Communicating about grammar: A task-based approach. *TESOL Quarterly, 25*, 605-628.

Fotos, S., Homan, R., & Poel, C. (1994). *Grammar in mind: Communicative English for fluency and accuracy*. Tokyo: Logos International.

Appendix A: Adverb Placement Task Sheet

Use only English during this group activity. One person should read the directions to the rest of the group.

Directions: Working in your groups, study the following sentences. These sentences contain adverbs, words that tell about the verb. In English sentences, adverbs can occur in several places:

Yesterday he studied English.
We *quickly* ate lunch.
He studied for the test *carefully*.

But adverbs cannot occur in one location in the English sentence. In groups, you must find that location—the location where English adverbs cannot occur. To help you solve this problem, you will ask and answer questions that contain these five adverbs: *yesterday, quickly, carefully, easily, often.*

1. First, decide who will start.
2. Then, that person asks the person to his or her right Question 1, and the person answers it.
3. Then, the person who answered Question 1 asks Question 2 to the person on his or her right.
4. Continue until everyone has asked and answered questions.
5. When people are answering questions, you should think about the location of the adverb. Do you think that the person is using the

adverb in the correct location? If not, tell the person where you think the correct location is.

6. When everyone has finished, discuss four general rules for adverb placement.
7. When you agree on the rules, write the rules at the bottom of this page.
8. When you are done, you may turn off your tape recorder.

Question 1: What did you do *yesterday*?

Question 2: Many people can solve mathematical problems *quickly*. How *quickly* can you calculate?

Question 3: Are you the type of person who prepares for examinations *carefully*?

Question 4: Some people remember what they read *easily*. Other people *easily* learn sports. What activities can you *easily* do?

Question 5: What type of activity do you *often* like to do? How *often* do you do this activity.

General Rules for Adverb Placement in English:

1. Adverbs may occur _____ .
2. Adverbs may also occur _____ .
3. And adverbs may also occur _____ .
4. However, adverbs may not be used _____ .

Appendix B: Relative Clause Task Sheet and Task Cards

Today's task is about making sentences with who, whom, which, *and* that. *In English, phrases with these words are called* relative clauses. Speak only English during this exercise. *One student should read the directions.*

Directions: Taking turns, read your task cards. Each task card gives one rule, and correct and incorrect sentences showing the rule. The student who reads the rule and sentences must then make his own sentence. The sentence should show the rule. The students should write down all of the rules, and then take turns making sentences for each rule.

Rule 1:
Rule 2:
Rule 3:
Rule 4:

Task Card 1

Rule 1: When the relative clause goes with the subject of the sentence, it should be near the subject, not at the end of the sentence.

Correct:　The boy who is five years old is very clever.
Incorrect: The boy is very clever who is five years old.

Now, make your own sentence using this rule.

Task Card 2

Rule 2: Don't leave unnecessary pronouns in the sentence, and don't forget to use *who, whom,* or *which.*

Correct:　The boy who likes English speaks well.
Incorrect: The boy who he likes English speaks well. (*he* is unnecessary)
Correct:　I like flowers which bloom in spring.
Incorrect: I like flowers bloom in spring (*which* has been forgotten)

Now make your own sentence using this rule.

Task Card 3

Rule 3: Don't use the wrong pronoun. *Who* and *whom* are for people, *which* is for things. *That* is often used with people or things.

Correct:　The dictionary which is on the table is mine.
Incorrect: The dictionary who is on the table is mine.
Correct:　The girl that just stood up is my friend. The book that is on the table is mine.

Now make your own sentence using this rule.

Appendix C: Relative Clause Pre-/ Posttests

> **Task Card 4**
>
> Rule 4: Questions with relative clauses can begin with *who* and end with *to* or can begin with *to whom*. Both are correct. But be careful not to use *to* twice.
>
> Correct: Who did you give the book to? To whom did you give the book?
> Incorrect: To whom did you give the book to? (*to* is used twice)

Now make your own sentence using this rule.

Relative Clause Objective Section: Grammaticality Judgment Test
Students should indicate which sentences are correct and which are incorrect.

_____   1. The sandwich tastes good which she made.
_____   2. The sandwich which she made tastes good.
_____   3. The student who I spoke to understood English well.
_____   4. The student who I spoke to him understood English well.
_____   5. He likes girls who are cheerful and kind.
_____   6. He likes girls which are cheerful and kind.
_____   7. The boy and the dog which were lost were found today.
_____   8. The boy and the dog that were lost were found today.
_____   9. The father son is my friend went to America yesterday.
_____ 10. The father whose son is my friend went to America yesterday.
_____ 11. The baseball player who is best on the team hit the home run.
_____ 12. The baseball player hit the home run who is best on the team.
_____ 13. Who did Taka give the book to?
_____ 14. To whom did Taka give the book?
_____ 15. To whom did Taka give the book to?
_____ 16. The man who Yuki gave the present to was her boyfriend.
_____ 17. The man to whom Yuki gave the present was her boyfriend.
_____ 18. To whom did you lend the money to?
_____ 19. Who did you lend the money to?
_____ 20. To whom did you lend the money?

Relative Clause Sentence Production Test

Students should make as many single sentences as possible by combining the two short sentences, into one long sentence. They must use *who, whom,* or *which.*

1. The cake tastes good. Taka made the cake.
2. The students passed the examination. The students entered this school.
3. The girl was going shopping. I spoke to the girl.
4. I gave my seat to the man. The man got off the train.
5. The woman was her aunt. Mari sent a letter to the woman.

Contributors

Sandra S. Fotos is Associate Professor at Shenshu University, Tokyo, Japan. Christopher Jon Poel is Assistant Professor of English at Musashi Institute of Technology, Tokyo, Japan.

Grammar Targets

Levels
Advanced

Aims
Explore logical
relationships of ideas
while stressing the
interdependence of
grammar and meaning
in a sentence
Become familiar with
people or events that
have influenced history
and share information
about native countries

Class Time
30 minutes

Preparation Time
20–30 minutes

Resources
Any encyclopedia
Overhead projector
(OHP)
One pen and one
transparency/student

S tudents create sentences using specific grammar targets.

Procedure

1. Choose a person or event.
2. Read an encyclopedia article (or article in a newspaper or magazine) about the person or event.
3. Outline the person's life or the event briefly.
4. Make a copy of the outline for each student or use an OHP to show an outline to the class.
5. Briefly discuss the outline, adding historical or personal background and allowing students to do the same.
6. Give each student (or pair of students if the class is large) a transparency with a different grammar target, and ask the students to write a sentence that is both grammatically and semantically accurate.
7. Share the sentences on the OHP, encouraging self-correction and student-based revision suggestions. (See Appendix for a sample outline with suggested grammar targets.)

Caveats and Options

1. Assign students to write several more sentences about the information, using teacher-assigned targets or allowing students to choose their own targets.
2. Assign students to write an outline about a person or event from their own country's history who might be similar to the selected person's contribution (e.g., a famous chemist, politician, actor, educator). At

the end of their outlines, students should include the grammar targets they think can be used to create good sentences.

3. Have students exchange papers and write sentences for each other.
4. Once you have developed several outlines, you'll have flexible materials that can be changed and used for different targets. Outlines for national holidays or special local celebrations are particularly interesting for students.

Appendix A: Sample Outline

Harriet Tubman 1821?-1913

1821 born as a slave on a plantation in Maryland
      parents illiterate—could not record birth
      worked as a slave in a field

1844 married John Tubman
      Tubman was a freed black
      Harriet questioned morality of slavery
      two of her sisters sold
      she was beaten brutally
      decided to escape
      traveled north by night, hid by day
      arrived in Philadelphia
      worked as a cook
      decided to return to Maryland to rescue slaves
      used North Star as a guide
      in 12 years traveled south 19 times

1857 brought her parents to freedom
      slave owners offered 40,000 dollars for her capture
      never learned to read or write
      became speaker at antislavery meetings

1861 volunteered to help North during Civil War
      worked as cook and spy for Union Army

1865 moved to New York
      founded home for elderly blacks

1913 died

Appendix B: Sample Grammar Targets

Directions: Based on information about Harriet Tubman, write a sentence containing this grammar on your transparency. Be particularly careful to avoid any major grammatical errors. Remember, you may not change the capitalization or the punctuation of the target. Pay close attention to punctuation.

Relative Clauses Targeted

1. who
2. , who
3. that
4. , which
5. whose
6. whom
7. for whom
8. , where
9. , some of whom
10. when

Singular/Plural Nouns Targeted

1. A lot
2. quite a few
3. some
4. Each
5. every
6. The number
7. None
8. all
9. One of
10. quite a bit

Modal Verbs Targeted

1. could have
2. should not have

3. must not have
4. might have been
5. would go
6. had to
7. may rather have
8. must have been
9. ought to have
10. would have liked

Combination Exercise

1. , so
2. ; therefore,
3. Even though
4. nor
5. what
6. would have been
7. Traveling
8. Had she
9. to be
10. The more

Contributor

Susan Kasten is Instructor in the Intensive English Language Institute, University of North Texas, in the United States.

UNO

Aims
Increase awareness of
word class, word stress,
and their relationship
while practicing the
pronunciation of words
with difficult stress
patterns

Class Time
20 minutes

Preparation Time
5 minutes

Resources
A packet of word cards
and some special UNO
cards

Students work on word stress and recognizing word class in a card game format.

Procedure

1. Prepare lists of four-syllable words with various stress patterns, selecting words from different word classes. An example of this can be seen in Appendix B. There should be a total of at least 40 words to make the game enjoyable.
2. Put these words on poker-sized cards to form a set of at least 40 cards. Include the special UNO cards to increase the fun of the game.
3. Ask students to sit around a table.
4. Shuffle the set of cards as if playing poker. Give each student a set of five cards and then put the rest of the pack face down on the table.
5. Turn over the first card of the pack and put it on the table to show the word.
6. The players take turns to play the game, with the objective of giving out all the cards in their hands. Each time, the player has to give out a card either with the same word class (noun, adjective . . .) or with the same stress pattern as the word on the table. If the student cannot find one, he or she has to draw another card. If he or she has one, he or she says the word while giving the card out.
7. Monitor the game and correct any misuse of word stress or incorrect recognition of word class, penalizing the player by making him or her take two more cards from the table.
8. The player who has only one card in hand after giving one out when it is his or her turn has to call out "uno" or "last card," which signals to other players that he or she is going to finish the game unless they adopt strategies to prevent it.

9. The first player to have given out the entire hand of cards wins, while the rest of the players can continue to play until every player has finished with their cards.

10. Special UNO cards add fun to the game. These should be of a very limited number, say, just one or two sets in the whole pack. When the player holds one of these cards, he or she can give it out at any time. When a player gives out Card A, the next player is penalized by having to pick two more cards. When a player gives out Card B, the next player must pick four more cards. With Card C, the next player misses a turn, whereas Card D changes the direction of flow of turns from a clockwise to a counterclockwise direction, or vice versa.

Caveats and Options

1. This game is best played with three to six players, or, alternatively, three to six pairs. Pairing up students for the game can be helpful for a weaker class, as advice from a partner can reduce hesitation and help the players develop greater confidence.

2. Words to be put on cards are up to your discretion. Three- or five-syllable words, or words with an assortment of syllables and stress patterns work well.

3. With a big class, students not playing can learn from watching others play. The last two students or pairs of students to get rid of their cards are regarded as losers and have to remain in the game to compete with new players.

4. Word stress and word class often have a predictable relationship. Even advanced students, however, often fail to place the correct word stress on words when they appear in a word class different from their more frequently occurring counterparts. Common problem words include *explanatory* and *distributive*, where students tend to place the stress as they would for their corresponding nouns. Similarly, for *preferable* and *maintenance*, they tend to place the stress as for their corresponding verbs. This activity is designed to heighten students' awareness of the relationship of words of different grammatical categories to their stress patterns.

5. This game mimics the popular card game UNO, or, when played with poker options, The Last Card. It is very easy to play and is fun for learners of all ages and levels.

6. One good thing about the game is that with the penalties, weaker students have more opportunities to practice, and they retire from the game only when they have shown evidence of mastering words recurring in the pack of cards.

7. The game can be adapted to provide an activity for almost any two aspects of grammar which can be cross-tabulated into a table like that of Appendix A (e.g., one for vocabulary recognition at an elementary level, with different kinds of places cross-tabulated with different kinds of jobs; or at a very advanced level, with mood (indicative, declarative, imperative, and interrogative) cross-tabulated with language functions (stating, requesting, and asking for information), in which case sentences will be written on cards and the student player is expected to read the sentences with the appropriate intonation as well). The possibilities are endless.

Appendix A: Table of Words

	DA di di di	di DA di di	di di DA di
Noun	magnetism intimacy temperament commentary	vitality efficiency economist prosperity	contribution recognition composition exposition
Adjective	generative vulnerable preferable legendary	contributive indifferent original intestinal	advantageous extramural maladjusted insufficient
Adverb	diligently competently meaninglessly culturally	submissively dependently abusively dishonestly	incorrectly inexactly insecurely imprecisely
Present Participle	criticizing advertising sympathizing realizing	establishing distributing developing continuing	undeleting disregarding overflowing undermining

**Appendix B:
Sample UNO
Cards**

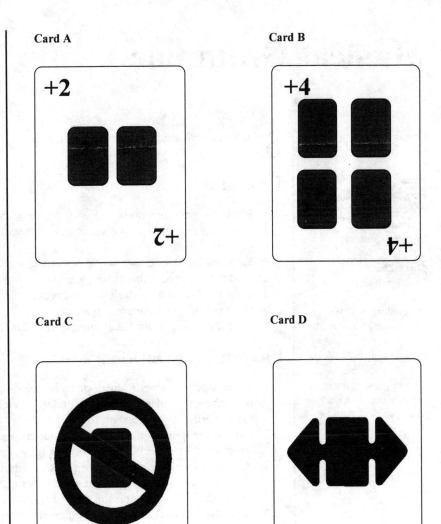

Card A

+2

+2

Card B

+4

+4

Card C

Card D

Contributor

Bruce Ka-cheung Ma is Lecturer in English in the College of Higher Vocational Studies at City Polytechnic of Hong Kong.

Musical Grammar

Levels
Any

Aims
Contextualize and review grammar points in a memorable listening context

Class Time
15–20 minutes

Preparation Time
20–30 minutes

Resources
Any personal music library; good sources are the works of Elton John, Jackson Browne, Woody Guthrie, Bob Dylan, Peter, Paul and Mary, Joan Baez, or Simon and Garfunkel

S ong lyrics provide grammar reinforcement.

Procedure

1. Present a grammar point that will be the focus of the exercise.
2. Hand out prepared music cloze exercise with focal grammar points deleted.
3. Students listen to music while reading along.
4. Students complete the cloze exercise.
5. Elicit the answers to the cloze exercise.
6. Students listen to the song again.
7. Pose questions about the grammar or content of the song.

Caveats and Options

1. When studying a verb tense, provide the simple form of the verb in parentheses to make a cloze exercise. Students provide the appropriate verb tense according to the text.
2. Provide the lyrics of the song. The students underline the grammatical structure they have been studying as they hear it.
3. Provide no written lyrics. Have the students write down the item(s) they have been studying as they hear them.
4. The students could retell the text of the song.
5. Have the students correct any grammatical errors and write out the full forms of contractions or colloquialisms they find in the song.

Contributor

Virginia Martin teaches ESL in the English Department, Bowling Green State University, Ohio, in the United States.

Inductive and Deductive Consciousness-Raising Tasks

Levels
Low intermediate–
intermediate

Aims
Solve grammar
problems deductively
(applying rules to data)
as well as inductively
(using data to formulate
rules)

Class Time
1 hour

Preparation Time
1-2 hours

Resources
Grammar textbooks and
references (see
References and Further
Reading)

This contribution offers (a) activities to develop deductive thinking through rule-driven tasks in which learners are taught specific rules for a grammar structure that they then apply to sentences and (b) inductive thinking through data-driven tasks in which learners examine data illustrating the structure in question and then discover the rules.

Procedure

1. Choose the grammar structure, either by observing student errors or by following the order of presentation in an existing textbook or syllabus.
2. Decide whether the task should be deductive or inductive. Deductive tasks are said to be rule driven in the sense that students are given rules for a structure and are asked to apply those rules to some sentences (see Tag Question Task in Appendix A). In contrast, inductive tasks are data driven, meaning that the task starts out with examples that illustrate the target structure.

   The examples typically contain both grammatical sentences and ungrammatical sentences that reflect common errors. The goal of this type of task is for students to formulate a rule for using the structure (see Article Task in Appendix B). Deductive tasks are appropriate for structures that are relatively difficult or have complex rules. Inductive tasks can be used when the structural patterns are easier for learners to pick out or the rules are relatively simple.
3. Organize the classroom as needed for carrying out the task. For example, for pair work, desks should be arranged so that students can sit face-to-face without being able to see each other's task sheet.
4. Set up the task through a routine warm-up, explanation of the procedure, directions, or preteaching.

5. As they work on the task, circulate among the learners (or groups), ensuring that everyone is on target, and providing assistance to those who might need it.

6. If you notice that many of the students are having similar problems, it may be necessary to pause and offer a teacher-fronted explanation or minilecture to help them past the difficulties.

7. Upon completion of the task, a wrap-up session should follow. This session can focus on problems you noticed during task performance, student questions, correcting the task sheet, or other group activities. If a pre-/posttest evaluation is being used, the posttest can be given at this point. It is also possible for classes that meet for a longer period (e.g., 90 minutes or 2 hours) to have an interactive wrap-up in which learners from different groups offer comments and corrections to one another, much like peer tutoring is used in writing classes.

8. Another useful wrap-up activity is to discuss the actual performance of the task, focusing specifically on how well the pair or group did this time and what they can do to improve their performance in the future.

9. If you notice that students are still having problems with the structure, present addtional tasks focusing on the problem areas in subsequent lessons.

Caveats and Options

1. While these two types of tasks are designed with the communicative classroom in mind, it is possible to use them in other situations as well. For example, when using deductive tasks, you may wish to introduce the rules for the structure in a more traditional lecture style lesson before going on to a task. When inductive tasks are used, it is possible to have the students work individually with the data followed by discussion of the rules in a teacher-fronted grammar lesson.

2. Tasks in general, and consciousness-raising grammar tasks specifically, take a lot of preparation. One big advantage, however, is that tasks can (with relatively minor adjustments) be used over and over with different groups of students.

3. It is necessary to keep in mind that one task (or even one series of tasks) is not enough to ensure that students will learn the structure;

follow-up activities are necessary. These follow-up activities may be additional tasks, formal grammar lessons, or communicative activities designed to enhance and expand the students' knowledge. For example, the Tag Question Task in Appendix A is only one task in a series. The complete series includes a game, a worksheet, and a jigsaw task in addition to the task presented here. (The complete task can be obtained by writing to the authors.)

4. Another important consideration to keep in mind is that tasks are often unfamiliar to learners. Be prepared for unforeseen problems or confusion, especially if this is the first time they have used tasks.

References and Further Reading

Celce-Murcia, M., & Larsen-Freeman, D. (1983). *The grammar book.* Cambridge, MA: Newbury House.

Ellis, R. (1992). *Second language acquisition and language pedagogy.* Cambridge: Cambridge University Press.

Fotos, S., Homan, R., & Poel, C. (1994). *Grammar in mind: Communicative English for fluency and accuracy.* Tokyo: Logos International.

Nunan, D. (1989). *Designing tasks for the communicative classroom.* Cambridge: Cambridge University Press.

Appendix A: Deductive Consciousness-Raising Task—Tag Questions

1. A tag question is a question added to the end of a sentence which makes that sentence into a question. For example:

   Mary went shopping. → Mary went shopping, *didn't she?*
   The boys aren't playing. → The boys aren't playing, *are they?*

2. Making tag questions is not so difficult if you follow these rules:

   a. If the sentence is positive, add *not* in the tag question.
      Example: She *went* to the store, *didn't she?*
      If the sentence is negative, remove *not* from the tag question.
      Example: He *didn't drink* too much last night, *did he?*
   b. The pronoun in the tag must match the noun in the subject.
      Example: *Steve* is coming to the party, isn't *he?*

    c. If there is a helping verb in the sentence, use it in the tag.
       Example: The calendar *is* on the desk, *isn't* it?
       If there is no helping verb, then use *do*.
          Example: Mr. Jones *drives* a Toyota, *doesn't* he?

3. In the letter below, all of the tag questions are wrong. Circle each tag question and then explain what is wrong with it. If you have trouble, look at the three rules.

Friday, May 13

Dear Suzie,

  I got your letter in the mail today and I couldn't believe what you'd written. You really haven't decided to move out of your parents' house, did you? Your parents didn't really say I was no good, did I? You haven't really started dating another man, haven't you? Your new boyfriend doesn't really want you to marry him, don't you? You haven't forgotten our engagement, haven't you? My mother didn't really tell you to return the engagement ring, was she? I haven't made you that angry, did I? We are going to be lovers again, aren't they? You will come and talk to me about this little problem, can't I? We can still be friends, aren't we? Please write back as soon as possible.

Love, Freddy

P.S. You do still love me, do you?

  Remember, you don't have to correct the mistakes—just explain why they are wrong.

Appendix B: Inductive Consciousness-Raising Task—The Articles *a* and *the*

Story-Making Lesson

Part 1: Work with your partner. Read the sentences on the cards to each other and try to make a story from them. Be very careful about the order of the sentences. When you decide on the order, write down the story. Pay careful attention to the use of *a* and *the*. Do not show your cards to your partner.

One day in English class, the teacher (Mrs. Smith) had to leave the classroom for a minute. Before leaving, she told the class to study the textbook while she was gone. But, the students didn't study. Here's what happened as soon as Mrs. Smith left.

(On the actual worksheet, leave lines for the students to write their sentences.)

They all quickly sat down. When Mrs. Smith came back, she saw all the students studying hard. She was very pleased with her good students.

(Print Part 2 a separate sheet or on the back of the worksheet for Part 1.) Part 2: Again, work with your partner. Look at the sentences you wrote in Part 1. What do you notice about the use of *a* and *the*? Can you write two rules?

Rule 1: We use *a* when _____.
Rule 2: We use *the* when _____.

Sentences for Task Cards (Note: Distribute cards as follows: Student A— No. 2, No. 3, No. 5, No. 8; Student B—No. 1, No. 4, No. 6, No. 7. The cards should not be numbered when you give them to the students.)

1. A boy wearing a striped shirt went to the door to watch for Mrs. Smith.
2. Mrs. Smith was gone, so the boy told his friends it was OK.
3. John, who was sitting at his desk, made a paper airplane.
4. He threw the airplane to a friend who was standing at the chalkboard.

5. The friend threw it back and then started drawing a picture of the teacher on the chalkboard.
6. Suddenly the boy at the door saw Mrs. Smith coming and he shouted.
7. The friend who was drawing on the chalkboard picked up a towel.
8. He quickly erased the picture and left the towel at the chalkboard.

Contributors

Christopher Jon Poel is Assistant Professor of English at Musashi Institute of Technology, Tokyo, Japan. Sandra S. Fotos is Associate Professor at Shenshu University, Tokyo, Japan.

Cloze Listening With Student-Generated Texts

Levels
Any

Aims
Focus on forms in discourse and match spoken and written English, while reviewing previously presented and practiced grammar

Class Time
3–10 minutes

Preparation Time
30 minutes

Resources
Writing tasks or assignments you usually give in class

This cloze exercise reviews previously introduced grammar points based on students' own written texts.

Procedure

1. Review students' responses to a homework assignment or in-class writing task you have given them, and select one or more responses. (This works best when the task is a dialogue or a brief narrative or expository piece.)
2. Type up the student text(s), double-spaced, editing for grammar errors and leaving blanks for the relevant grammar features to be practiced (e.g., if you are working on verb tenses, leave out the verbs; if prepositions, leave out the prepositions.) Number every fifth line for reference when checking. Make a copy for each student.
3. In class, hand out the copies, indicating that the material was written by classmates. Read the text three times at a normal rate: The first time, students just listen while reading the text in front of them; the second time, students write in the missing words or expressions that they hear—just pause at the end of each sentence giving time to write; and the third time, students read over the text again, filling in or changing any blanks they have missed.
4. Provide immediate feedback on "right answers" so that students can check their own papers and ask about items they don't understand. Answers can be provided in various ways: Students can call them out and you can write them quickly on the board or an overhead transparency; students can write them on the board, and so on.

Caveats and Options

1. This activity can be used to practice any grammar feature. It works well with verb forms, modals, prepositions, phrasal verbs, comparative expressions, and is especially good for forms that are discourse sensitive.

2. If you have a series of short paragraphs, you could do the exercise a paragraph at a time.
3. If the texts are very short, you can simply dictate the entire text and save the preparation time. However, this changes the activity from an explicit focus on one grammatical feature to a more global dictation task. (See Celce-Murcia & Hilles, 1989, on dictation.)

References and Further Reading

Celce-Murcia, M., & Hilles, J. (1989). *Techniques and resources in teaching grammar.* Oxford: Oxford University Press.

Nunan, D. (1989). *The learner-centered curriculum.* Cambridge: Cambridge University Press.

Ur, P. (1985). *Listening comprehension.* Cambridge: Cambridge University Press.

Appendix: Sample Exercise

(This exercise is for a high intermediate-level class. It focuses on present tense verbs that do not take the progressive.)

Directions: Find a picture of a product (e.g., a food, beverage, cosmetic, or soap product) or draw a picture of a product. Write an advertisement for your product using some verbs of sensory perception (e.g., *smell, taste, look, see, hear, seem*). Continue your advertisement by adding three testimonials about your product. Use some verbs which describe mental perceptions and emotions.

(Student text prepared for cloze listening activity:)
Try Gratin Instant Food. It _____ fresh, it _____ fresh, and it _____ delicious. You can _____ it in one minute. It is convenient and also _____ money. Gratin is your only choice. Arnold Schwarzenegger says: "After you _____ it, you will be strong like me." Jane Fonda says: "I _____ this food. You can eat a lot and still _____ in good shape." Arsenio Hall says: "I _____ this is the best snack I've ever tasted."

Contributor

Patricia A. Porter is Professor of English and ESL Coordinator in the Department of English Language and Literature at San Francisco State University, California, in the United States.

Making Sense

Levels
Intermediate +

Aims
Analyze syntax

Class Time
50 minutes

Preparation Time
15 minutes

Resources
Copies of
"Jabberwocky" for each
student

Coherence and parts of speech are reviewed using the nonsense words of Lewis Carroll's "Jabberwocky."

Procedure

1. Make a copy of "Jabberwocky" with the unknown words underlined and the stanzas divided into two clearly labeled sections. Section A includes Stanzas 1-2, and Section B Stanzas 3-6. This division just about equally distributes the 28 unknown words (discounting repetition) between the two sections. The last stanza—a refrain of the first—is omitted or left to stand on its own.
2. Divide the class into groups of four or five students and call them Teams A or Teams B.
3. Provide each student with a copy of the poem.
4. Read the poem aloud.
5. Assigning Section A of the poem to Group A and Section B to Group B, ask the groups to identify the part of speech for each underlined unknown word in their section and to provide a rationale for each identification.
6. Allow 10-15 minutes of group discussion.
7. Moving around the A groups, have individual students report on their groups' conclusions. For each word, check whether or not other groups agree. If there is disagreement, lively discussion should follow. Repeat the process with the B groups.
8. When each unknown word has been labeled, have the whole class read the final stanza aloud with full dramatic effects.

Caveats and Options

1. After labeling the unknown words, students assign them meanings before being given those provided by Humpty Dumpty in *Through the Looking Glass*.
2. With prompts from you, students could play with the words. For example, they could try to determine how the removal of *did* affects the verbs *gyre* and *gimble*.
3. Discussion could expand to words around the unknown ones (e.g., how they know that *back* (Line 20) is not being used as a noun.
4. This is a light-hearted activity best used as a reinforcement tool. It serves as a review of, for example, tenses, linking verbs, articles, and noun modification. Most importantly, though, it empowers students. By controlling nonsense words, they see, often with amazement, the control they have of sense words.

References and Further Reading

For the works of Lewis Carroll, see

Carroll, L. (1982). *The complete illustrated works of Lewis Carroll.* New York: Avenel Books.

Carroll, L. (1982). *The Penguin complete Lewis Carroll.* Harmondsworth, England: Penguin.

Contributor

Margaret Shabka is Director of the English Language Program, University of Maryland Baltimore County, Baltimore, Maryland.

Grammar Consciousness Raising Through Contrastive Analysis

Levels
Intermediate +;
heterogenous classes

Aims
Work out aspects of
English grammar in
relation to L1
Develop an awareness
of the underlying
principles of contrastive
analysis

Class Time
45-60 minutes

Preparation Time
None

Resources
Bilingual dictionaries

In this problem-solving activity, students explicitly compare and contrast English with their L1.

Procedure

1. Explain the principles of cross-linguistic influence (CLI), in particular what used to be called negative transfer. Do this in the most practical and accessible terms possible by using examples from the L1s represented in class. You might use the difference in the use of prepositions in English and other languages and the many collocational rules for verbs in English, which so often differ from those of other languages.

   This preliminary session prepares students to perceive certain grammatical problems in terms of CLI. The goal is for students to learn how to work out for themselves certain grammatical aspects of English in terms of the similarities and contrasts between it and their L1.

   The first step is to introduce the general tendency for learners to associate some particular element of English with a counterpart in their L1 (abbreviated here as C). Next, they need to understand that this association is only valid in certain restricted contexts. For example, it is natural for beginning francophone learners of English to associate the French word *dans* with the English word *in* and then to overgeneralize it to inappropriate contexts, producing errors such as *He took* [something] *into his pocket* because the French use *dans* in this context. Ideally, the teacher should try to give as many examples as possible in order to cover all the languages represented in the class.

2. Introduce the specific problem of the focal item—in this case, *in*. As indicated above, the first step involves establishing in the students' minds what is the C of *in*. To do so, write *in* by itself on the board and ask the students to write down their own L1 counterpart for *in*.
3. Next, hand out sheets with the following examples. What you include in this list will, of course, depend on which uses of *in* you wish to cover. This particular list is quite exhaustive but could be reduced considerably.

Your umbrella is in the classroom.
The horses are in the field.
The ideas in this book are difficult to understand.
There are lots of fish in this river.
I read it in the newspaper.
I saw him in the morning/afternoon/evening.
I went there in the month of May.
She arrived here in 1992.
We'll raise the problem in the meeting.
I have a pain in my leg/stomach/neck . . .
In that case, I think we should stay at home.
I did my homework in the classroom.
In Question 10, you have to remember that the gender of the speaker is very important.
I can't remember the date, but it's in my notes.
There's not a cloud in the sky.
I hope she's in heaven.
I arrived just in time for class.
Don't worry, in time you'll almost forget her and only think about her every other day.
We're going to meet again in 2 weeks' time.
He is in France.
She's in the hospital for an operation.
I like living in the country.
He's in bed.
She's in school.
He came to the party in slippers (other articles of clothing).

I found it in the street.
I saw her in the crowd and I will never forget her face.
In my childhood, I lived with my grandparents.
I'll be ready in five minutes.
I like swimming in the sea.

Ideally such a list should be compiled with the L1s of the students in mind. In the case of this list, Item 12 might look like a repetition of the use of *in* in 1, and for most L1s, it probably is. However, for Japanese speakers, it is not. The choice of preposition in Japanese depends on the opposition between stating the position of something and stating the place in which an action takes place.

4. The students examine the uses and decide in which cases the use of *in* is equivalent to their C. This will permit them to make an initial statement such as: *My C is equivalent to* in *in Sentences (numbers given).*

   Ideally, as students become more sophisticated in using the strategy, they should be encouraged to generalize from the specifics of the sentence. For example, instead of simply mentioning Sentence 10, they might state: *When talking about parts of the body, use* in.

5. In a later step, the students examine those uses of C outside of the examples given. This will permit them to make a second, limiting statement such as: *However, when C is used in the following contexts (the students give the examples in their L1), the English equivalents are . . . .*

6. In the final step, the students examine those uses of *in* in the list which are not equivalent to C and decide on the equivalents in their L1s. This will permit them to make a statement such as: *Those uses of* in *in examples (numbers given) have the following equivalents in my L1 . . . .*

   Taking the example once again of francophones learning English, the three statements would be something like the following (the statements are not exhaustive and are only given as examples):

   a. *Dans* is equivalent to *in* Examples 1-4, 11, 12, 15, and 25-30.

b. However, *dans* is equivalent to *into* in contexts such as *He went into the room* and *within* in contexts such as *The village is within the borders of the town*.

c. In Examples 9, 10, 13, 18, 21, 22, *in* is equivalent to *à*. In Examples 16 and 23, *in* is also equivalent to *à* but it appears in the form of *au* because of the masculine determiner.

d. In Examples 7, 8 and 20, *in* is equivalent to *en*.

e. In Example 5, *in* is equivalent to *sur*.

In order to achieve such an analysis, students will need to use bilingual dictionaries. While they are doing so, you can circulate to encourage students to make generalizations rather than only refer to specific cases.

Caveats and Options

1. Carrying out such an exercise is of limited use unless there are follow-up activities. I would suggest that the first should entail the students' studying and learning from their analyses followed by some sort of written test.

2. This strategy works best with a heterogeneous class because of the different analyses entailed with different L1s. Where students share the same L1, teachers may provide the contrastive information themselves if they prefer a teacher-fronted deductive approach. However, the problem-solving strategy proposed here is equally applicable to such classes. Alternatively, one can use both approaches with the occasional problem-solving activity providing for a change of pace and a possibly more stimulating lesson.

3. The strategy seems best suited to those situations where there is the initial association between C and an element in English. It is therefore ideal for use with prepositions and collocational rules. It is inappropriate where there is no C, as is the case for articles in relation to Japanese, which does not have the determiners *a* and *the*.

4. The technique may be applicable in the case of some verb tenses. For example, the difference in meaning between the simple and progressive future tenses is often a cause of error, partly owing to negative transfer. Both Arabic and Japanese speakers, for example, tend to overgeneralize the use of the simple future with *will* because it is this

form which they initially associate with their own verbal forms used for indicating intention, and neither language has an equivalent for the prospective future with *going to*. However, attempting the proposed strategy with problems related to the complexities of the present perfect, for example, and other such difficulties should be approached with some caution.

5. If this strategy is used as a regular activity, it is advisable that students use a separate notebook to compile a permanent record of their contrastive analyses.

References and Further Reading

Gass, S., & Selinker, L. (Eds.) (1983). *Language transfer in language learning*. Rowley, MA: Newbury House.

Kellerman, E. (1983). Now you see it, now you don't. In S. Gass & L. Selinker (Eds.), *Language transfer in language learning*. Rowley, MA: Newbury House.

Sheen, R. (forthcoming) The advantage of exploiting contrastive analysis in language teaching. *International Review of Applied Linguistics*.

Von Elek, T., & Oskarsson, M. (1973). *Teaching foreign language grammar to adults: A comparative study*. Stockholm, Sweden: Almquist & Wiksell.

Contributor

Ronald Sheen teaches in the Faculty of Education at Tottori University, Tottori, Japan.

Drawing Meaning Out of Grammar

Levels
Low intermediate +

Aims
Contrast grammatical
patterns visually

Class Time
1½ hours

Preparation Time
30 minutes

Resources
Paper, pens, glue

Students draw distinctions between grammatical structures to help themselves visualize grammatical patterns such as *be/get used to* (*accustomed to*) and *used to* (past repeated action, completed) and restrictive/nonrestrictive relative clauses.

Procedure

1. Students working in pairs or threes create a pair of imaginative sentences that contrast particular grammatical structures:

   a. I used to collect earthworms.
   b. I'm used to collecting earthworms.

   a. The students, who like gambling, went to Atlantic City last weekend.
   b. The students who like gambling went to Atlantic City last weekend.

2. Students design a simple picture to illustrate each of the two sentences that will distinguish one from the other.

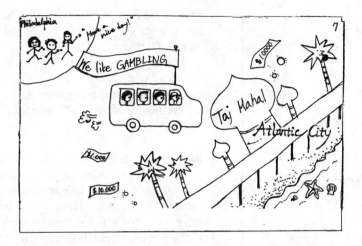

Occasionally, a pair of students may need to be talked through the differences or given a hint about how to illustrate their sentences. However, it is better if they can do this on their own, as the purpose of the activity is to have them visualize the difference. Students who may feel they are not artists may need to be encouraged: Even simple stick figures are fine.

3. Once rough sketches of the picture concepts are finished, students transfer the pictures to the blank card forms, one picture per blank. Lines should be dark enough for photocopying.
4. On both of the other two blank forms, students should print neatly the contrasting pairs of sentences. Writing should be dark enough for photocopying. (If photocopying facilities are not available, the one set of cards may be used, rotating sets of pictures in the review activity.)
5. Check the cards and number the pictures.
6. Photocopy enough copies for one set per pair or group of students so students will be able to see all pictures/sentence pairs in a review activity.

7. Students cut out pictures and phrases and glue them onto the cardboard rectangles, picture on one side, pair of sentences on the other.
8. Review activity:
   a. Students working in pairs or small group try to match the sentences with the pictures.
   b. The class compares answers.
   c. Problem pictures and sentences are discussed in class.

Caveats and Options

1. Save sets of cards for use with another class. Build up a collection of Drawing Meaning Out of Grammar cards.
2. In a 10-week course, this activity might be done only once or twice, but not on a regular basis as the novelty may wear thin. Once you have collected sets for other patterns, these can be used for simple, enjoyable exercises in lieu of the full production of cards.

Acknowledgments

Ho Il Kang and Mariko Izumo supplied the illustrations.

Contributor

Margaret van Naerssen is Adjunct Lecturer in ESL and teacher training at the University of Pennsylvania and Immaculata College, in the United States.

Part X: Editing and Revision Activities

Editing the Word Processor Way

Students learn to check their written work for sentence completeness and subject-verb agreement, using a word processor to reformat and edit.

Procedure

Levels
Intermediate–high intermediate

Aims
Become more conscious about written grammar while learning how to use a word processor for editing

Class Time
1 hour

Preparation Time
None

Resources
Computers
Word processing system

1. The student brings a computer file of his or her written work to class or types a piece of his or her own written English onto the computer during class. This sample should be at least a paragraph in length and formatted correctly. The sample should have been revised for meaning and content prior to undertaking this editing stage of the writing process.
2. The student reformats the sample into individual sentences and numbers each sentence separately (see the example in the Appendix).
3. The student then uses one of the following methods for marking the complete subject and the complete verb of each sentence:

   a. Using the word processing system, he or she underlines the complete subject once and the complete verb twice.
   b. If the printer used with this system does not print double underlining, then the student should put a single line under the complete subject and bold lettering for the complete verb.

   After marking the sentences, the student prints a copy of the sample for analysis and saves the sample to a disk for later editing.

4. Working with the printed copy, the student decides if each sentence is complete. If the sentence is not complete, the student indicates the problem and attempts to correct it. The student is free to discuss the sentences with other students and with you.

217

5. The student decides if the subject and the verb of each sentence agree with each other. If there is a problem, the student corrects it. Again, the student is free to discuss the sentences with other members of the class.

6. After making the corrections to each sentence, the student removes the numbers and reformats the sentences into the standard paragraph format. A clean copy of the sample is printed and stapled together with the original for the student to keep. When the activity is repeated, the student can compare the errors and corrections of the first activity with those of the second to see if he or she has made any improvements or is continuing to have difficulties with the same areas of sentence grammar.

Caveats and Options

1. Students can work individually, in pairs, or in small groups. For example, two students can work together to edit each other's writing. Each student provides a sample of writing for the editing process. Working together on one sample at a time, the students decide on the analysis of the sentences as in Step 3. After both samples have been marked for complete subject and compete verb, the students can work individually to decide if changes are needed in their own writing, or they can continue to work as a pair. I recommend doing the activity individually at first and then in pairs for follow-up.

2. Students can deal with written text as sentences more easily when they can see them separately. This process also forces them to make decisions about which words go with which sentences that they sometimes avoid through comma splices or run-on sentences.

3. This process can be used with graduate students in a teacher preparation course, by having them reformat examples of ESL student writing to analyze the sentence-level grammar. Graduate students, some of whom are experienced teachers, can often see what is happening in students' sentences more clearly when they are reformatted than they can in traditional paragraph format.

Appendix: Sample Student Paragraph

Leaving one's house in the morning and getting on the expressway is like entering a zoo. There the driver find all types of personalities from completely "crazy" all the way to "shy." Is as if all the insecurities, problems, anxieties and stresses are placed on that poor steering wheel of the car.

Reformatted Paragraph

(The subject is underlined and the verb is bolded.)

1. Leaving one's house in the morning and getting on the expressway **is** like entering a zoo. (no errors)
2. There the driver **find** all types of personalities from completely "crazy" all the way to "shy". (need to adjust either the subject or the verb for agreement)
3. **Is** as if all the insecurities, problems, anxieties and stresses are placed on that poor steering wheel of the car. (need to add subject)

Contributor

Patricia Byrd is Associate Professor in the Department of Applied Linguistics/ESL, Georgia State University, in the United States.

Grammar Journals

This journal activity enhances students' written grammar and proofreading skills, with the goal of promoting independence and editorial control in the students' future writing.

Levels
Any

Aims
Receive ongoing, consistent grammar feedback and learn a system for logging correct grammatical forms and word usage
Activate passive knowledge of grammatical structures for use in writing
Learn proofreading skills

Class Time
Little

Preparation Time
45 minutes

Resources
English dictionary and grammar reference book recommended

Procedure

1. Explain the journal procedure and hand out a copy of the journal guidelines and list of grammar correction symbols to each student. Any set of symbols can be used, but a simple system works well at the intermediate and advanced levels as it puts the burden of correction on the students and is less time consuming for teachers (see Appendix).
2. Introduce proofreading skills, explain why proofreading is important, and demonstrate how to do it effectively. If time allows, give students a chance to practice in class before proofreading at home on their own.
3. Assign for homework a journal entry on an assigned topic. Topics can come from a variety of sources. Students can be asked to summarize and respond to an article or passage that they have read or a video they have watched. Alternatively, they can be assigned to report on a topic that has been discussed during a pair or group activity.

   Topics which are related to the content in a reading, listening, or speaking class are particularly successful because students will be familiar with the topic and relevant vocabulary. Personal topics are not recommended for this type of journal as students may discuss painful events or personal problems, making grammar correction difficult or insulting.

4. Ask the students to proofread their entries and hand them in for comments. While proofreading, they should pay particular attention to grammar points covered in class and to error corrections made to previous entries. (Proofreading can be assigned for homework or done as an in-class activity.)

5. After collecting the journals, read each entry twice, first for content, then for grammar. Respond to the content in the form of an endnote by commenting on the students' opinions, sharing your own experiences, and answering any questions that have been posed. Then give a grade for thoughtfulness and effort. For simplicity, a ✔+ , ✔, ✔- and system can be used, though a letter or number system is also possible.

6. During the second reading, look for grammatical errors and, using a different color pen, insert in-text symbols where errors occur. Based on your preference, class proficiency level, and course focus, you will need to decide which errors to mark. You may want to address all errors, those errors which have been addressed in class, or only those occurring frequently within a student's writing.

   In addition to the in-text symbols (and using the same color pen), you may want to add summary grammar comments. You can point out specific rules or areas for individual focus, such as *"Even though is always two words,"* or "In your next entry, please check your punctuation carefully." You and your students can refer to these comments easily—students, to obtain accurate grammar information for future use, and teachers, to ensure that students are applying their suggestions to future entries. At this point in the procedure, do not grade students on their grammar usage.

7. After the entries are returned to the students, they must do two things: reread what they have written, and then correct the areas which have been marked.

8. Next, collect the journals again, read the students' self-corrections, and supply corrections for improperly corrected or uncorrected text. At this time, give a grade for the quality of their grammar corrections, not their initial grammatical accuracy. Here, too, a ✔+ , ✔, ✔-grading system works well.

9. Finally, after the journals are returned, the students should use a highlighter to mark the grammar points that they want to remember. They can highlight grammar rules or corrections that have been provided by the teacher or corrections that they have made themselves. This procedure allows for easy reference because the highlighted grammar information appears in the same notebook where future entries will be written.

Step 9 completes one entry cycle. You may want to complete one cycle before assigning the next journal topic, or assign students to correct a previous entry and write a new entry at the same time.

Caveats and Options

1. Each week, present a particular grammar point for students to focus on when writing their journals. Choose journal topics that will elicit these forms. For example, after a lesson on the past tense, assign students a story to summarize using the past tense.
2. Though this type of journal is somewhat time-consuming for teachers, it is effective in promoting grammatical accuracy. It provides students with an opportunity to hone proofreading skills and to develop a system for recording useful grammar information. Most importantly, it brings great satisfaction to students, especially at the end of a course, when they look back and see the progress they have made.

Appendix: Sample Journal Entry

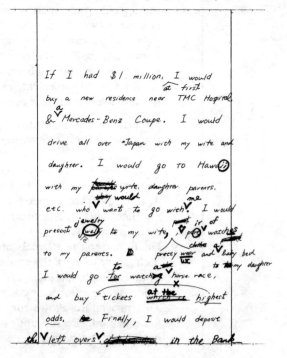

Kazuhiko,
You sound like a very generous man! I'm sure your parents, wife, and daughter would be very happy to receive the gifts you have mentioned. Be careful at the horse races! ✓+

grammar corrections = ✓+

Contributor

Amy Hemmert, formerly Instructor in the English Language Program, International Christian University in Tokyo, Japan, now resides in San Francisco, California, in the United States.

Competitive Sentence Correction

Levels
Any

Aims
Practice editing for
grammar and usage
errors
Raise consciousness
about editing strategies
and grammar rules by
collaborating to
determine the best ways
to correct sentences

Class Time
30 minutes–1 hour

Preparation Time
None

Resources
Students' homework

Students compete in teams to identify and correct errors from their written work.

Procedure

1. This game is best played on days you plan to return students' written work. Choose a number of faulty sentences from the students' written work that contain representative, problematic, or amusing errors in grammar, usage, or style. It's best to choose sentences with more than one error and in which the error(s) make the meaning of the sentence ambiguous (to challenge the students and impress on them the extent to which grammar and usage contribute to meaning).
2. Divide the class into two (or more) teams and have the teams arrange their chairs in circles for discussion. Write one of the faulty sentences you have chosen on the board, leaving room for each team to write their alternative versions of it.
3. Give students a time limit (2 or 3 minutes, perhaps longer for more difficult sentences) to discuss the sentence with their team members and to agree on an alternative. When the time limit is up, one student from each team writes their version on the board. (The representative may be appointed by the team or the teacher, or the team members may take turns.)
4. Evaluate the sentences to determine which is the "best" correction. Although you are the final judge, team members can be called upon to justify their decisions, especially in cases in which both sentences are correct but differ in style or meaning. The team whose sentence is judged the best is awarded a point. (When both sentences still contain errors, you may choose to award neither team a point or to award the point to the lesser of two evils.)

Caveats and Options

The value of this simple exercise is that it uses competition to get students interested in how they approach editing. The evaluation period at the end of each round often yields fruitful discussion about the best or most efficient ways to identify errors.

Contributor

Rodney Jones is University Assistant Lecturer in the English Department, City Polytechnic of Hong Kong.

A Democratic Paragraph

Levels
Beginning–intermediate

Aims
Review basic grammar
rules for sentence
structure, word order,
word forms, and
agreement
Practice the use of
transitional words and
expressions
Recognize the value of
revising

Class Time
One or two 50-minute
classes

Preparation Time
Varies

Resources
Students' sentence-
combining homework

Students work in groups to decide which of their combined sentences should be selected to create a class paragraph.

Procedure

1. Assign for homework a sentence-combining exercise that requires students to join short simple sentences into longer complex sentences and then to join those into a coherent paragraph by adding linking words and phrases.
2. Form groups of three to six students. To manage time, it is best to have no more than four groups. The students go through their homework sentence by sentence. Each student reads his or her sentence, and the group chooses the best sentence or decides to combine the best features of several students' work. The chosen sentences are written on the board.
3. When the whole sentence is on the board, the group proofreads it and makes further improvements, always based on the consensus of the group.
4. The small groups then regroup as a whole class and compare their various products. They create one final paragraph by taking the best features of each group's work.

Caveats and Options

1. Larger groups may be formed, but it is harder to reach consensus; also, it is best to have an uneven number in the groups.
2. With beginning students, single sentences rather than paragraphs can be used.

3. With advanced students, free paragraphs on the same topic can be used, though it is harder to create a single final paragraph. The exercise can be used to demonstrate the possible varieties of sentence structures, points of view, and organizational patterns as well as correctness of basic grammar.
4. This process works well with students from cultural groups who are group oriented and dislike being called on individually.

Contributor

Janan M. Malinowski is Lecturer in ESL in the General Education Division of Hawaii Community College, Hilo, Hawaii, in the United States.

Correct Me If I'm Wrong

Levels
Any

Aims
Identify errors in a text

Class Time
10 minutes

Preparation Time
30 minutes

Resources
Copy of a paragraph to
be read aloud
Whiteboard or
chalkboard on which to
keep score

As training for editing their own written work, students try to catch errors in a paragraph read aloud by the teacher.

Procedure

1. Prepare a paragraph that contains several errors. These errors can be points that have just been taught (e.g., using the past tense instead of the present tense for low-level classes) or a mixture of different types of errors (e.g., vocabulary/clause relationship/sentence structure for high-level classes).
2. Ask the class to listen to the paragraph you are about to read aloud. Tell the students that the paragraph contains several errors. Whenever the students hear an error in the story, they must raise their hands. Tell them that you will keep score on the board—one column for them and one for you.
3. Begin reading the story. Try not to give the students any clues when you reach an error, that is, do not slow down, hesitate, or emphasize the errors.
4. If the students identify an error, give the class a point. If they can correct the error, give them another point. If the students do not identify an error, give yourself a point.

Caveats and Options

1. This exercise is a good lead-in to peer correction.
2. As a follow-up activity, students can exchange some written work they have done and help each other identify errors.
3. This exercise gives students active practice in identifying errors and can help them focus their attention on particular aspects of a text.

Which aspects to focus on depends on what you wish to emphasize in the paragraph that is used as the model for correction.

Contributor

Lindsay Miller is University Lecturer in the English Department, City Polytechnic of Hong Kong.

Three-for-One Student Transcripts

Levels
Low intermediate +

Aims
Become more aware of
own language use and
difference between
actual use and
knowledge of rules
Offer teachers rough
draft transcripts for
checking or testing
semi-naturalistic use of
language and for
research purposes

Class Time
40–50 minutes

Preparation Time
1 hour

Resources
Short interviews,
information-gap
activities, cartoons,
pictures
Colorful advertisements

Students record themselves performing interactive tasks, then make transcripts to find their own errors.

Procedure

1. Students do an interactive or open-ended individual task with written instructions. No writing should be done in preparation for the task which should produce about 2-3 minutes of actual recorded speech per student. Longer recordings will not be practical, given the time needed for transcribing, self-correction, and teacher follow-up.

   For example, working in pairs, without looking at each other's half of the ad, the students try to find out what differences there are in the two pictures, talking for about 3-5 minutes. This elicits determiners and other noun modifiers.

2. Students record themselves. To make listening and recording easier when using headphones with microphones, move the earphone slightly off the ear opposite the microphone side; the headphone will stay on.

3. Students then transcribe only their own language, including all mistakes, transcribing on every other line.

4. Students correct their own transcripts, putting corrections on blank lines, and do not erase previous mistakes.

5. Students rewind their tape to the beginning of the task and turn the tape and transcript in to the instructor.

6. The instructor listens to the tape while reading along with the transcript.

7. The instructor checks for the appropriate use of the focus of the task and makes additional corrections as necessary.

Caveats and Options

If class size does not permit listening to all tapes each time, a sampling of different tapes each time can be done, and yet all transcripts can still be checked.

Acknowledgment

I was influenced by one of Tracy Terrell's testing techniques.

Contributor

Margaret van Naerssen is Adjunct Lecturer in ESL and teacher training at the University of Pennsylvania and Immaculata College, in the United States.

Also available from TESOL

Pronunciation Pedagogy and Theory:
New Views, New Directions
Joan Morley, Editor

Video in Second Language Teaching:
Using, Selecting, and Producing Video for the Classroom
Susan Stempleski and Paul Arcario, Editors

For more information, contact

Teachers of English to Speakers of Other Languages, Inc.
1600 Cameron Street, Suite 300
Alexandria, Virginia 22314 USA
Tel 703-836-0774 ● Fax 703-836-7864